History of Islamic Economic Thought

ISLAMIC ECONOMICS INSTITUTE

The Islamic Economics Institute (IEI) – originally known as the Islamic Economics Research Center – was established in 1977 at King Abdulaziz University (KAU), Jeddah, Saudi Arabia. In 2011, it was upgraded into an institute that interactively combines research, teaching, and training in one location.

KAU, established in 1967, is a public university covering a wide range of subjects in 24 different faculties. About 75 of its teaching programs are internationally accredited. In 2014, KAU ranked as the best university in Saudi Arabia and the 49th in Asia by Times Ranking.

The IEI mission is to produce knowledge and design programs for researchers and experts in the field of Islamic economics, and to observe and accommodate contemporary needs of the society.

Researchers are the main source of IEI successes, since its inception. IEI is not just limited to the in-house full-time researchers; it has been building a wide network of researchers worldwide specialized in different topics in the field of Islamic economics. One of the IEI researchers received the King Faisal International Prize in 1982. IEI itself and four of its researchers have been awarded the Islamic Development Bank Prize in Islamic economics. In addition, one of the current researchers at IEI is a laureate of the King Faisal International Prize.

IEI has been a research-based institution for almost four decades. At the same time, it has been involved in designing teaching curricula for different courses in the field of Islamic economics since 1985. In 2013, IEI launched its first two-year degree in Islamic Finance, namely the Executive MA in Islamic Finance.

Training is the third pillar for IEI. It should play an important role by bridging the gap between research and teaching by encouraging real-life case studies. Four different international training programs have been launched since 2012 and offered in Jeddah for MA students and for executives from Europe and other parts of the world.

Since 1983, IEI has published the first journal in the field of Islamic economics, the *Journal of King Abdulaziz University – Islamic Economics*. It is a biannual peer-refereed journal. The journal is listed in three international databases: the *Journal of Economic Literature, SCOPUS – Elsevier,* and *Thomson Reuters*.

Sheikh Saleh Kamel Library is a specialized library in the field of Islamic economics at IEI. It contains more than 33,000 titles. A special section is devoted to recent PhD and MA theses in the field of Islamic economics. Abstracts and table of contents of these theses are made available at the IEI website to encourage new research in the field.

In collaboration with University Paris 1 Pantheon-Sorbonne, IEI at KAU established a research Chair for Ethics and Financial Norms at University Paris 1; to allow for a deeper study of ethical principles and financial norms.

The Saudi-Spanish Center for Islamic Economics and Finance (SCIEF) is an academic collaboration between the Business School at IE University and IEI at KAU. The SCIEF is created exclusively for research, education, executive training and consultancy, and to promote Islamic economics and finance internationally.

History of Islamic Economic Thought

Contributions of Muslim Scholars to Economic Thought and Analysis

Abdul Azim Islahi

Islamic Economics Institute, King Abdulaziz University, Saudi Arabia

In Association with the Islamic Economics Institute at KAU

Edward Elgar

Cheltenham, UK • Northampton, MA, USA

Published by
Edward Elgar Publishing Limited
The Lypiatts
15 Lansdown Road
Cheltenham
Glos GL50 2JA
UK

Edward Elgar Publishing, Inc.
William Pratt House
9 Dewey Court
Northampton
Massachusetts 01060
USA

A catalogue record for this book
is available from the British Library

Library of Congress Control Number: 2014947225

This book is available electronically in the ElgarOnline.com
Economics Subject Collection, E-ISBN 978 1 78471 138 2

ISBN 978 1 78471 137 5

Typeset by Servis Filmsetting Ltd, Stockport, Cheshire
Printed and bound in Great Britain by T.J. International Ltd, Padstow

Contents

Foreword

It is with a real feeling of gratification that I write the foreword to Professor Islahi's work *History of Islamic Economic Thought.* This work is among Professor Islahi's continuing efforts exploring the history of Islamic economic thought. The book highlights contributions of Muslim scholars to economic thought, an area which deserves more attention by economists.

The book has been prepared in response to a quest for a common ground for dialogue among civilizations in the field of economics. So, it documents the multidimensional linkages and influences between the Islamic civilization and medieval European culture, particularly in the area of economic thought. Muslim scholars' influence on medieval Europe with respect to philosophy, science, mathematics, medicine, geography, history, art and culture is well-documented and known in the circles of concerned subjects. But their impact on economic thinking and institutions is yet to be fully explored and recognized. The present work is a serious attempt in this direction. Professor Islahi also notes the changing trend in recent years of Western scholars towards Muslim contribution to economics and growing admission of indebtedness to the Muslim intellectual heritage in the European renaissance. This tendency will not only bridge the gap in history of economic thought left by earlier writers, but will also increase understanding between the East and the West and facilitate interaction at academic and intellectual levels.

The Islamic Economics Research Center, now the Islamic Economics Institute, has an unmatched history of supporting research work on the history of Islamic economic thought and it has produced a number of studies on the subject. The present book by one of the researchers at the Institute is another landmark in this series. I am confident that it will, by Allah's will, be of great help for teaching and researching on history of economic thought in general and Islamic economic thought in particular in universities all over the world.

Abdullah Qurban Turkistani
Dean, Islamic Economics Institute
5 May 2014

Preface

The present study explores and analyzes economic ideas of Muslim scholars up to the fifteenth century and defines various phases of the development of economic thought in Islam. It seeks to determine their role in the evolution of mainstream economics and to find out their impact on the scholastic scholars and mercantilists. It also discusses various channels through which their ideas reached the European West and served as the link between Greek philosophers and scholastic economists. It provides materials that can be used to make up existing deficiency – the great gap in evolution of economic thought – persisting in the literature on the subject.

An earlier work on this subject by this author was published about a decade ago under the title *Contributions of Muslim Scholars to Economic Thought and Analysis*. The present study, though it follows the structure and approach of the original work, incorporates new information, improves many ideas and develops some parts of the earlier work. In particular, I have made considerable additions in the last three chapters of the book which enhance achieving the objective of this line of study. I have also updated and greatly increased citations to books in the bibliography. Most importantly, I have added many new names of past scholars and their works which I came across after publication of my earlier book. They are now over 100 in total. I hope inclusion of additional references on the subject will help readers as well as promote further interest and research in this area which has not been paid proper attention in the past. I have adopted an eclectic approach in this study and hope that this will generate curiosity among the readers to further investigate and carry deep and detailed study of the works of past scholars. It may also draw their attention to the works of Muslim scholars in later centuries that largely remain unexplored.

It is both customary and proper for an author to thank those who assisted him and at the same time to absolve them of any responsibility for remaining errors. Unfortunately, it is no longer feasible to list the names of all those people who have helped me out with their expertise and knowledge at various stages of this work. However, I wish to thank in particular Professor Muhammad Nejatullah Siddiqi, Professor Ishtiaq Ahmad Zilli and Professor Munawar Iqbal. I must also express my gratitude to Dr Mohammed Najeeb Ghazali the former Director of the Islamic Economics Research Center, and Dr Abdullah Qurban Turkistani, Dean of the Islamic Economics Institute, for their extraordinary help and generous support for preparation and publication of this book.

All praise belongs to Allah and Allah alone. I bow my head before Him in gratitude for enabling me to complete this work.

Abdul Azim Islahi
Jeddah
20 April 2014

1. Introduction

1.1 MISSING LINK IN THE HISTORY OF ECONOMIC THOUGHT

A search for solutions to economic problems has been a common concern of all societies. This is the cause of economic thinking. Economic practices existed long before there was any theorizing on the subject. Members of human society thought over economic problems in isolation, in closed societies or together with the other groups, and were influenced by their thinking and ideas. Interaction and convergence of thought provided the necessary basis for continuity of sciences and development of ideas. Thus, economics 'evolved historically from many minds and temperaments' and economic thought is 'a cumulative accretion of human knowledge' (Ekelund and Hebert, 1983, p. 3). No doubt, a sense of common heritage brings various groups closer and gives rise to mutual understanding and due regard to each other resulting into cooperation and joint efforts to refinement and furtherance of such thinking and research in these areas. It also provides a suitable environment for cultural dialogue between various nations that fell apart with the passage of time. With this objective in mind it would be interesting and, hopefully, also fruitful to investigate the contribution of various nations to development of economic thought and analysis. The present study aims to discuss contributions of Muslim scholars that played an important role in continuity and growth of mainstream economics.

There is an increasing awareness now that the 'root of modern economic analysis extends much further back in time than a good many contemporary students of economics are led to realize' (Gordon, 1975, p. xi). But even those writers who realize that history of economic thought is 'a continual progression of ideas made up of epochal contributions of new list of knowledge added to the accumulated legacy of the past' (Ekelund and Hebert, 1983, p. 4), leave a gap in their writings and feel no concern to support their stand by facts.[1] The present study aims to provide material that could be used to make up the existing deficiency in the literature on history of economic thought. By reporting and analyzing economic ideas of Muslim scholars, it will also explore various channels through which their ideas reached the European West and influenced the scholastic scholars. Thus, they became part, though yet to be recognized, of the family tree of economics. It is hoped that this would strengthen the feeling of the unity of knowledge and an acknowledgement that may enhance mutual understanding and cooperation. The work addresses historians of economic thought in general and students of Islamic economic thought in particular. It also seeks to draw attention of those who are in search of common grounds in sciences and culture for mutual understanding and cooperation.

1.2 LITERATURE REVIEW

Since the very beginning, writers on history of economic thought have tended to ignore contribution of Muslim scholars to the subject. The economic historians start with the Greek philosophers and Roman jurists and administrators. They also mention opinions of some Christian fathers who lived in the early centuries of the Christian era. Then they jump to the middle ages when Europe came out from darkness to light and thinking on different natural and social sciences began, leaving a wide gap of about five centuries. This was exactly the period when Muslims ruled the greater part of the known world, established powerful empires, developed economies and contributed to the promotion of culture and science including economics.

Modern development of Islamic economics began during the second quarter of the twentieth century. Writings on the contribution of Muslim scholars of the past were part of this development. Perhaps the first article to introduce economic thought of Muslim scholars was written by Salih (1933) in Arabic entitled 'Arab Economic Thought in the Fifteenth Century' in which he discussed economic ideas of Ibn Khaldun,[2] al-Maqrizi,[3] and al-Dulaji.[4] Next, al-Hashimi (1937) published his paper on 'Economic Views of al-Biruni'[5] again in Arabic. The same year Rifʿat (1937) wrote on 'Ibn Khaldun's Views on Economics' in Urdu. The first paper in English was written by Abdul-Qadir (1941) entitled 'The Social and Political Ideas of Ibn Khaldun'. And the first Ph.D. on the subject was awarded by Cairo University to Nash'at (1944) on *Economic Thought in the Prolegomena of Ibn Khaldun*, written in Arabic.

In the first half of the twentieth century most of the works on economic thought in Islam were written in Urdu or Arabic. Moreover, they were authored by non-professionals and only a few were in English, so they remained unnoticed by the mainstream conventional economists.

Joseph Schumpeter (1997, pp. 73–4) talked of 'the great gap' in evolution and development of economic thought in his monumental work

History of Economic Analysis, first published posthumously in 1954. Siddiqi (1964) writing on economic thought of Qadi Abu Yusuf[6] ten years after publication of Schumpeter's work took notice of that assertion.[7] 'Economic Thought of Islam: Ibn Khaldun' by a distinguished Western economist, Spengler (1964), drew the attention of the historians of economic thought to explore further in that direction.[8] By surveying *Muslim Economic Thinking* of the past and present up to 1975 (Siddiqi, 1980) and survey of 'Recent Works on History of Economic Thought in Islam' in 1982, Siddiqi supplied more material for researchers.[9] In 1987, Mirakhor penned down a well-documented paper in which he questioned the Schumpeterian great gap thesis and pointed out to the 'serious omission in the history of economics of profound contribution made by Muslim scholars'. He showed that 'both motive and opportunity existed for the Medieval European scholars to be influenced by the economic ideas and institutions developed in medieval Islam and that based on the available evidences, they availed themselves of such an opportunity by using some of the available knowledge to advance their ideas' (Mirakhor, 1987, p. 249). The echo of this paper was heard at the History of Economics Society Conference in Toronto, Canada, June 1988 in which Ghazanfar (2003, p. 19, footnote 1) presented his study on 'Scholastic Economics and Arab Scholars: The Great Gap Thesis Reconsidered'. The so-called gap in the economic thought motivated this writer in a joint work with Ghazanfar to show that a substantial body of contemporary economics is traceable to Muslim scholastics such as al-Ghazali[10] and others (Ghazanfar and Islahi, 1990). Ghazanfar (1995, p. 235) further reinforced it in his paper 'History of Economic Thought: The Schumpeterian "great gap", the Lost Arab-Islamic Legacy and the Literature Gap'. While 'disputing the validity of the great gap thesis', the author has shown by survey of some major works on the subject, that the literature gap is 'manifest in almost all relevant works in economics'. Hosseini (2003) also refuted the Schumpeterian Great Gap in an article entitled 'Contributions of Medieval Muslim Scholars to the History of Economics and their Impact: A Refutation of the Schumpeterian Great Gap'.

In the meantime, a number of works appeared in English and Arabic that dealt with the economic ideas of individual Islamic scholars who lived in the period attributed as the blank centuries of economic thought.[11] These works may not have touched on the great gap thesis, but the very existence of a number of writings relating to the period was sufficient to discard it.

Our purpose in this study is to present a comprehensive picture of the development of economic thought in Islamic tradition right from the beginning up to roughly the first-millennium Hijrah. The Muslim civilization and its intellectual and political power, after reaching its zenith, had by the early tenth/sixteenth century begun to show clear signs of decadence while the Western renaissance was in full swing. It was the time when writings on how to achieve economic progress and strengthen the country through foreign trade took the form of a movement in the West, known as *mercantilism* in economic literature. This, as we shall see below, was reaction against the Muslim conquests in the battlefield. At that stage of history, the Muslim scholars, after transmitting Greek ideas along with their own additions and interpretations, to the world at large, gradually receded into oblivion.

1.3 SCHEME OF THE STUDY

We shall distinguish three broad phases of the development of Islamic economic thought and Muslims' contributions. The first phase is formation period; the second phase is translation period; and the third phase is re-translation and transmission period. While presenting the nature and characteristics of each phase we shall take note of the representative scholars of each phase.

Next we shall systematically and extensively discuss various economic concepts that were analyzed or improved over Greek ideas by the Muslim scholars. It will be a straight-line development of concepts and ideas with reference to those who had a part in formulating those ideas. Being the main theme of this work, the Islamic tradition in economic thought spreads over many chapters.

We shall also examine the impact of the Muslim scholars on the Western scholastics in the medieval period and various channels through which it passed.

Some textbooks give a family tree of economics science and its growth in diagrammatic form but they overlook the part played by the Muslim scholars in development of mainstream economics. We shall study a few such trees in Chapter 8 and point out the place of Islamic economics in the family tree of mainstream economics.

As will be clear from our analysis, the Western scholastic scholars borrowed a lot from Muslim scholars but they seldom acknowledged it. We shall examine reasons for that.

But the trend is changing now. In recent years some writers have acknowledged contributions of the Muslim scholars to economic thought and analysis and there is growing admission of indebtedness to the Muslim intellectual heritage in the European renaissance. This is a healthy sign and praiseworthy development that should be welcomed by all. We shall conclude our study by surveying such remarks. We hope that this would encourage those who are still hesitant to acknowledge contributions of the Muslim scholars to economic thought. We are optimistic that such efforts will open a cultural dialogue and create a sense of affinity and regard for past ideas as a common heritage of humankind.

NOTES

1. We find remarks such as 'it is inconceivable that there was no economic thinking over so many years - even in the Dark Ages', (Newman et al., 1954, p. 15) or statements like 'Historians of economic doctrine now recognize that modern theory is the product of continuous growth over a much longer period of time than was previously assumed' (Langholm, 1998, p. vii), but no trouble is taken to investigate economic thought in the gap period to establish continuity and substantiate this rightful claim.
2. Abd al-Rahman Ibn Khaldun (732–808/1332–1406) (Ibn Jaldun in Spanish and Ibn Haldun in Turkish) was born in Tunis and died in Egypt, where he was settled during the last years of his life. He played a pivotal role in the politics of North Africa and Spain. His work *Kitāb al-'Ibar* is of unrivalled value as a source of reference to the history of Arab and non-Arab nations until his time. His brilliant work *The Muqaddimah: An Introduction to History*, considered the most sublime and intellectual achievement of the Middle Ages, is a treasury of many sciences like history, psychology, sociology, geography, economics, political sciences, etc. Franz Rosenthal translated it into English in three volumes, first published in New York in 1958 by the Bollingen Foundation, and an improved edition in 1967 by the foundation and Princeton University Press, Princeton, NJ.
3. Ahmad b. Ali al-Maqrizi (766–845/1364–1442). Born and lived in Egypt, with a multifarious career. Famous for historical works, dealt with questions of social history such as weights and measures and coinage. Some important works by him are *'al-Khiṭaṭ, al-Sulūk li Maʿrifat al-Mulūk, Imtāʿ al-Asmāʿ, Ighāthat al-Ummah bi Kashf al-Ghummah.* The last one has been translated and excellently edited with related additional information by Adel Allouche (1994) entitled *Mamlūk Economics*, University of Utah Press, Salt Lake City, UT.
4. Ahmed b. Ali al-Dulaji (770–838/1368–1435). Born in Dulajah, a city in Egypt, and died in Cairo, was author of many valuable works. His book *al-Falākah wa'l-Maflūkūn* [*Poverty and the Poor*] is of economic interest in which he addresses the poverty stricken people and discusses various manifestations of poverty and recommends remedy to get rid of it.
5. Abu Rayhan al-Biruni (362–442/973–1048). Born in what is today called Uzbekistan. The scope of his enquiries was vast and profound. With Sultan Mahmud Ghaznawi (361–421/971–1030), he traveled to India where he stayed for 12 years, learned Sanskrit and authored *Kitāb al-Hind* [*India*], which has been translated by Edward C. Sachau (London, 1914). Al-Biruni often compares Indian and Greek views.
6. Yaqub b. Ibrahim Abu Yusuf (113–82/731–98) the student of Abu Hanifah (81–150/700–767) and one of the co-founders of the Hanafi school of jurisprudence, became chief justice during Harun al-Rashid's era (170–94/786–809) the Abbasid Caliph, on whose request he authored *Kitāb al-Kharāj* [*The Book on Taxation*]. It is one of the earliest works on the Islamic system of taxation. Its text was first printed in Cairo in 1302/1885. It has been translated into many languages. Shemesh (1969) rearranged the text and chapters and published under the title *Taxation in Islam* only that part which is related to economic matters. A complete translation was done by Ali (1979), Islamic Book Centres, Lahore, PAKISTAN.
7. Much earlier, Frank Knight, the Chicago economist, while reviewing the book in the

Southern Economic Journal ((1955), **21**, 261–72) pointed out this deficiency of the work saying that 'if Schumpeter was writing to start with the Babylonians albeit with only a brief reference, he surely should have been able to make some, even if limited reference to Indian (and presumably other Asian) sources as well' (quoted by Mark Perlman in his 'Introduction', 1997, p. XXIII).

8. In the opinion of Professor Mirakhor (1987, p. 250) 'Although the paper is riddled with an "oriental attitude", it is a valiant effort by a distinguished historian of economic thought to deal, partially, with the economic thought of Islam. This indeed was the first attempt of its kind in the field. It contained a wealth of ideas for further research. However, the evidence suggests that this creditable work has been ignored by the profession.'
9. In addition to Siddiqi's works cited above, the Islamic Economics Research Center (now the Islamic Economics Institute), Jeddah, published some other books and research papers related to the history of economic thought in Islam such as (in chronological order):

    1. *Al-Islām wa'l-Nuqūd* [*Islam and Money*] by Rafic Yunus al-Misri (1981), 2nd edn (1990);
    2. *Economic Thought of Ibn al-Qayyim* by Abdul Azim Islahi (1984);
    3. 'Ibn Taimiyah's Concept of Market Mechanism' by Abdul Azim Islahi (1986);
    4. *History of Economic Thought in Islam: A Bibliography* by Abdul Azim Islahi (1997);
    5. *Economic Thought of al-Ghazali* by S.M. Ghazanfar and Abdul Azim Islahi (1998), 2nd edn (2011).
    6. *Fi'l-Fikr al-Iqtiṣādī al-Islāmī: Qirā'at fi'l-Turāth* [*On Islamic Economic Thought: Readings in the Heritage*] by Rafic Yunus al-Misri (1999);
    7. *Muslim Economic Thinking and Institutions in the 10th A.H./16th C.E. Century* by Abdul Azim Islahi (2009);
    8. *A Study of Muslim Economic Thinking in the 11th A.H./17th C.E. Century* by Abdul Azim Islahi (2011);
    9. *Islamic Economic Thinking in the 12th A.H./18th C.E. Century: With Special Reference to Shah Wali-Allah Al-Dihlawi* by Abdul Azim Islahi (2011).

10. Abu Hamid Muhammad b. Muhammad al-Ghazali (450-505/1058-1111), lived during the Saljuq period (429–707/1061–1299 CE). His scholarship extended to many diverse fields of learning. Most of his economic ideas are found in his famous work *'Iḥyā' 'Ulūm al-Dīn* and *al-Tibr al-Masbūk fi Naṣīḥat al-Mulūk*. For a detailed study of his economic ideas, see Ghazanfar and Islahi (1990) and (1998). He criticized philosophy in his work *Tahāfut al-Falāsifah*.
11. For such works one may refer to bibliographies prepared by Islahi (1997) in English and by Nuqli (1998) in Arabic. At the occasion of the Seventh International Conference on Islamic Economics, organized by King Abdulaziz University, during 1–3 April 2008, a research paper entitled 'Thirty Years of Research on History of Islamic Economics: Assessment and Future Directions ' was presented (Islahi, 2008[b]) in which the author studied and evaluated the research during 1976–2006. The finding is that hitherto the research in the history of Islamic economic thought has been dominantly language, region, and period specific – Arabic, the Middle East and up to the ninth/fifteenth century respectively. The paper emphasized the need for intensive and extensive research to include more personalities, ideas, periods, languages and regions, and to write a systematic comprehensive history of the subject.

2. Phases of the development of economic thought in Islam

2.1 REVEALED KNOWLEDGE: THE STARTING POINT

The history of Islamic economics goes back to the Qur'an and Sunnah. The Qur'an as the Word of God revealed to the Prophet Muhammad (peace be upon him), and Sunnah as his practical demonstration and explanation, contains a number of economic teachings and principles applicable to various conditions.[1] Thought is a product of human mind, whereas the Qur'anic teachings and prophetic explanations are divine in character. It is, therefore, the human interpretations and inferences and their applications in changing times, spaces and conditions that form the body of economic 'thought' of the people of Islam. The Muslim scholars accepted the economic teachings of the Qur'an and Sunnah as a starting point and used reason to solve problems in changing historical and economic conditions. They did not hesitate benefiting from the experience of other people. The process continued throughout Islamic history. In the period under study, we can divide the process into three broad phases:

1. First phase, the formation period covering the period just after cessation of the Revelation to the end of the Companions'[2] era (11–100 A.H./632–718 C.E.). (Henceforth the former figure would mean A.H. (after Hijrah) and the latter/C.E. (common era).)
2. Second phase, the translation period, when foreign ideas were translated into Arabic and the Muslim scholars got an opportunity to benefit from intellectual and practical works of other people (second–fifth/eighth–eleventh century).
3. Third phase, the re-translation and transmission period, when Greco-Arab Islamic ideas reached Europe through translation and other contacts (sixth–ninth/twelfth–fifteenth century).

2.2 FIRST PHASE: THE FORMATION PERIOD

Economic ideas, in written form existed long before the advent of Islam. The Greek ideas, especially, are considered as the fountainhead of conventional economics. However, Islamic economic thought, in its formation period, was not influenced by any outside elements. No doubt, since pre-Islamic times, the Arabs had some commercial relations with neighboring countries but they did not have cultural and intellectual contacts with them. There is no evidence of translation activities during that early period. Nor were means of communication so developed which could foster acquaintance with foreign ideas. Since the Qur'an and *Sunnah* contained a number of economic principles and many detailed economic teachings, there was no pressing need to look for guidance from outside sources. The early Islamic economic thought was based on its basic sources. The economic teachings found in the Qur'an and *Sunnah* were expanded by the Muslim scholars using *qiyās* [analogical reasoning] and *ijtihād* [fresh original thinking] and through their own perceptions and experiences.

The Qur'anic teachings on economic matters are broad and a few in number. The Qur'an mostly gives basic principles and stresses the use of reason for specific solutions. This led to the appearance of a chain of scholars who derived rules to solve new problems and created a juristic logic [*uṣūl al-fiqh*] applicable to a wide variety of social patterns. Their methodology was to refer first to the Qur'an and practices of the Prophet (pbuh) and precedents of his companions and immediate followers who were trained by him. Not finding anything there, they applied analogy and other inferred rules to deduce the *Shar'īyah* injunctions for the new situation. Gradually, a number of schools of thought in jurisprudence emerged. They were named after their leading scholars and creative thinkers [*imām* or *mujtahid muṭlaq*], most famous among them are (in chronological order) Zayd bin Ali,[3] Abu Hanifah,[4] Malik,[5] Shafi'i,[6] Ahmad bin Hanbal,[7] etc.[8] These schools of jurisprudence were firmly established within a period of less than 300 years after the Prophet (pbuh). The masses had faith in them and followed their path because they were experts of the basic sources of Islam and free from any alien influence. Reflection on economic issues was only one aspect of their rulings. People sought after their guidance for every day questions on religion. On economic issues they did provide some sort of analysis. The Islamic economic analysis owes a great deal to legal inquiry of this age.

Writings on economic topics and the collection of the Prophet's traditions on financial matters started by the end of this phase and in the early period of the next phase by the students of the leading jurists [*imams*] and their contemporaries. But due to the nature of their works, they can be considered part of this phase. For example, Abu Yusuf and Muhammad al-Shaybani[9] authored *Kitāb al-Kharāj* and *Kitāb al-Kasb* respectively. Yahya b. Adam al-Qurashi[10] compiled traditions of the Prophet related to taxes and other financial obligations, while Abu Ubayd al-Qasim bin Sallam[11] and later his student, Ibn-Zanjawayh,[12] authored *Kitāb al-Amwāl*. Ibn Abi al-Dunya[13] wrote on *Iṣlāḥ al-māl* and Abu Bakr al-Khallal[14] on business and economic activities in general.

The importance of this period will be clear if we have just a look at the economic ideas that were touched by Muslim scholars in the formation phase of Islamic economics. The following is an incomplete list of such ideas:

Market and its regulation, supply and demand, price fixation, money, credit and credit instruments, interest and commodity exchange, taxation, public finance, fiscal policy, various forms of business organizations, agricultural relations, *zakāh*, inheritance, property, poverty and riches.

Although some translation activities, as we shall note below, started as early as in the first/seventh century, they were of a different nature and had no discernible impact[15] on the evolution of economic theory. For one, they were insignificant in nature and remained restricted to the ruling elite only. Second, the Muslim scholars at this stage devoted fully to the study and development of *Sharʿīyah* sciences and did not feel the need for foreign sources. The development of economic thought in this period was inspired by the Qur'an and *Sunnah*.

2.3 SECOND PHASE: THE TRANSLATION PERIOD

By the translation period we mean the Age when foreign classical works and masterpieces, in particular, those embodying Greek ideas, were translated into Arabic and the Muslim scholars came to know about them. The translation activity started in the first century Hijrah itself although it took two more centuries to make its influence felt among the Muslim scholars. The first incidence of translation is reported during the Caliphate of ʿUmar.[16] Khalid b. al-Walid[17] advised the use of the *dīwān* [office or register]. He said to ʿUmar that he had seen the rulers of Syria keeping a *dīwān*. ʿUmar accepted the idea of Khalid. It has also been said that the person who advised ʿUmar to introduce the *dīwān* was al-Hurmuzan.[18] This took place in the year 20/640 (Ibn Khaldun, n.d., p. 112). Since the term '*dīwān*' is a Persian word, the latter is more plausible. However, the *dīwān*s of land tax collections remained in Iraq and Syria in Persian and Byzantine Greek respectively till the caliphate of Abd al-Malik b. Marwan[19] who ordered their translation into Arabic (ibid.). Later Khalid b. Yazid[20] made a systematic beginning of translation. He sent for scholars from India, Persia, Rome and Greece and arranged translations of their classical works. In the coming years the political upheavals interrupted this work. Its full-fledged commencement could be traced to the Abbasid Caliph al-Ma'mun[21] who established *Bayt al- Ḥikmah* [the house of wisdom] especially for this purpose (Hayes, 1983, p. 56). The incorporation of ancient sciences into Arabic gave a fresh lease of life to many important Indian, Persian and Greek works and saved them from oblivion.[22] In the words of Lewis (1982, p. 221), 'The great age of classical Muslim sciences was initiated by translations and adaptations of Persian, Indian and, above all, Greek scientific works.' The translation centers also proved a meeting point of East and West and a very effective channel to exchange of ideas. In coming centuries it facilitated even the transfer of Indian and Persian sciences to Europe. The case of Arab–Indian numerals is a living example of this intellectual exchange.[23]

By the end of third/ninth century, scholars were generally aware of and conversant with the contents of the translation works and they started exposition, assessment, addition and commentary on those sciences and even production of similar works. The major areas of translation included medicine, astronomy, art and philosophy and management of state and economy. Lewis admits: 'Muslim scientists added greatly to the material transmitted to them, through their own researches and through practical experiments and observations in fields as diverse as medicine, agriculture, geography, and warfare' (Lewis, 1982, p. 221). The movement of translations from alien sources came to an end around the fifth/eleventh century, but 'the development of Islamic science continued for some time beyond that' (ibid.).

2.3.1 Impact of Translations on Muslim Scholars

On clear examination it would appear that the translations of foreign ideas, did not fascinate all Muslim scholars equally. They took different positions towards imported ideas. At least three distinct streams can be identified.

a. First, those who rejected all Greek ideas altogether. The scholars in this group maintained that Islamic heritage of knowledge was sufficient for a safe and comfortable life. These alien sources would only confuse people and under their impact they would go astray. This group is generally referred to as 'traditionalist' or *muḥaddithūn*. Representatives of this group are al-Kinani,[24] al-Farra,[25] al-Sarakhsi,[26] etc.

b. The second group is the one who tried to distinguish between ideas that are beneficial and acceptable and those that are in contravention of the Islamic faith and principles. In case of conflict they tried to prove supremacy of the Islamic thought over the Greek thought or made an attempt to synthesize between the two if possible. They are variously known as Islamic scholastics, scholastic theologians, dialecticians or *mutakallimūn*. The representatives of this group are al-Mawardi,[27] al-Ghazali, Fakhr al-Din al-Razi,[28] etc.
c. The third group comprises those scholars who were deeply influenced by Greek ideas and philosophy and went too far to support, propound, and propagate them. They did not hesitate to interpret Islamic articles in such a way as to accommodate alien philosophical ideas. This group is referred to as 'Muslim philosophers' or *ḥukamā*. To this group belonged al-Kindi,[29] Ibn Sina,[30] Ibn al-Haytham,[31] al-Suhrawardi al-Maqtul,[32] Ibn Tufayl,[33] Nasir al-Din al-Tusi,[34] etc. However, it must be pointed out that the last three names do not belong to the second phase as they came after the fifth/eleventh century but due to the nature of their works we mention them with this group.

The Muslim philosophers translated treatises on *oikonomia* as '*ilm tadbīr al-manzil* [the science of household management]. It was one of the three branches of Greek philosophy, the other two being ethics ['*ilm al-akhlāq*] and politics ['*ilm al-siyāsah*]. As noted above, the Muslim scholars extended this branch of knowledge 'far beyond the household, embracing market, price, monetary, supply, and demand phenomena, and hinting at some of the macro-economic relations stressed by Lord Keynes (Spengler, 1964, p. 304). Ignoring these additions, the German scholar, Helmut Ritter states that '*the whole economic literature of Islam* can be traced to economics of Neo-pythagorean Bryson' (Heffening, 1934, p. 595, emphasis added). The unidentified Greek Bryson or Brason or Brasson (Brusson), whose work was unknown to the West (Spengler, 1964, p. 276 footnote) was, perhaps, first mentioned by him, which was picked up by some others.[35] There is no mention of Bryson in Schumpeter's encyclopedic work *History of Economics Analysis* which presents minute details of the history of intellectual efforts 'from the earliest discernible beginning' (Schumpeter, 1997, p. 3). The history of economic thought has numerous instances when an idea mentioned by a writer in the past re-emerged later with more details and clarity.[36] Moreover, certain ideas were developed simultaneously by different authors at different places without being aware of each other.[37] A mere resemblance between ideas of two persons does not necessarily mean that one has borrowed or copied from the other unless enough documentary evidence is available to that effect.

A fourth group may also be distinguished namely *sufi*s or *ahl al-taṣawwuf*. No doubt, elements of *sufism*, such as constant application to divine worship, complete devotion to Allah, aversion to the false splendor of the world, etc. are found in Islamic sources. But Islam advocated a balanced approach toward life. Ascetic behavior [*zuhd*] does not mean rejection of the worldly things. One can be an ascetic despite worldly affluence. It is true the other way round also. One can lack asceticism despite being poor (Ibn al-Qayyim, 1375 A.H., pp. 12–13). Once when the Prophet (pbuh) heard that some of his companions had vowed that they would not marry, not sleep and keep continuous fasting, he objected to their plea and told them that their attitude toward ascetism was imbalanced. He gave his own example that he, despite being the prophet of Allah, had married, was maintaining a family, slept and observed fasts occasionally (Ibn Hanbal, n.d., Vol. 3, p. 241.

However, in later centuries *sufism* became a cult and a movement, advocating a life of seclusion and denouncing all worldly means. Some *sufis* invented ideas and beliefs different from, or even contrary to the mainstream trend of Islamic thought. According to O'Leary (1968, p. 181), '*Sufism* which became prominent in the course of third century AH, was partly a product of Hellenistic influences.' 'As it is used in the history of Christian monasticism or of the devotees of several Indian religions, it implies a deliberate avoidance of normal pleasures and indulgences of human life, and especially of marriage, as things which entangle the soul and prevent its spiritual progress. In this sense asceticism is alien to the spirit of Islam' (ibid., p. 182). Islam presented a balanced mix of spirit and matter. This extreme spiritualism was a new phenomenon. 'Numerous theories have been put forward about the origin of this movement in Islam: Syrian monasticism, Neo Platonism, Persian Zoroastrianism, Indian Vedants' (Anawati, 1974, p. 366). Among the representatives of this group are Abd-Allah Harith b. Asad al-Muhasibi,[38] Junayd al-Baghdadi,[39] Abd al-Qadir al-Jilani,[40] al-Suhrawardi,[41] etc. Shedding the light on importance of this group in the history of economic thought, Siddiqi observes:

> The main contribution of *taṣawwuf* (or *zuhd*) to economic thought in Islam is a constant pull against giving too high a value to material wealth and a persistent push towards altruism and unselfish service of Allah's creatures. They emphasised the ultimate concern of the human soul and its reaching out towards its source in the Divine. They personally exemplified this concern by minimizing the material values and extolling the virtues and attributes that contributed towards felicity in the hereafter while also enabling the life here on the earth (Siddiqi, 1992, p. 15).

Even a fifth group of writers may be distinguished who combined the practical experience of business with Hellenic teachings and Islamic traditions. The representative author of this group is al-Dimashqi[42] who wrote *al-Ishārah ilā Maḥāsin al-Tijārah* [*The Guide to the Virtues of Trade*].

2.4 THIRD PHASE: THE RETRANSLATION AND TRANSMISSION PERIOD

The third phase of Islamic economic thought marks the translation of Islamic sciences in general and Greco-Arab sciences' (additions and commentaries of the Muslim scholars over the Greek philosophy) in particular from Arabic to Latin and other European languages. Durant (1950, p. 910) declares: 'The stream whereby the riches of Islamic thought were poured into the Christian West was by translation from Arabic into Latin.' We have reports regarding translation activities from Arabic to Greek by the end of the fourth century Hijrah in the Byzantine capital Constantinople[43] (Sezgin, 1984, p. 119). With the passage of time, the volume of retranslation work increased considerably. Hence the period before Western renaissance is termed as the 'translation age' (Myers, 1964, p. 78). As we shall discuss in Chapter 8, the translation work was only one of the numerous channels through which the Muslim scholars' contribution to economic thought and analysis reached the Western scholastics and became part and parcel of the mainstream economics. No doubt, 'the transmission of Greek economics to the West was the joint work of Christians, Muslims and Jews, who collaborated in harmony' (Grice-Hutchinson, 1978, p. 61). However, while mostly Christians and Jews helped in translation work from Greek to Arabic in the early period[44] and from Arabic to European languages in the later period,[45] it was Muslim scholars who mainly learned, discussed, analyzed and developed Greek thought.

In the two-way translation – to Arabic and from Arabic – the works of intellectual, philosophical and practical importance were given preference.[46] The works of *muḥaddithūn* [traditionalists] were hardly touched. Certain works of religious dialectics were translated as Christianity also faced the problem of conflict between religion and philosophy. They also wanted to establish superiority of religion over Greek philosophy or reconcile the two streams. In these efforts, works of the Muslim scholars, like al-Ghazali's *'Iḥyā' 'Ulūm al-Dīn,* were of great help.[47] Translation of the works of *ḥukamā'* [Muslim philosophers], physicians, scientists, and social thinkers dominated the scene. Works of Ibn Sina, al-Farabi,[48] Ibn Bajjah,[49] Ibn Rushd,[50] etc. were translated into Latin, Spanish, French, Hebrew and German languages. Grice-Hutchinson (1978, p. 71) writes:

> About the beginning of the twelfth century the Christian West began to awaken to the superiority of Islamic culture – or, perhaps we may better say, of Islamic technology, since the desire of Western Christians was not so much to enrich their intellectual heritage as to improve their performance in such practical activities as medicine, mathematics, arithmetic, astronomy, astrology, botany, torture and magic, in all of which the Arabs were known to be exceptionally proficient.

Although various European capitals organized translation of the work of the Muslim scholars, countries from where the Muslims were driven away – Sicily (late eleventh century) and Spain (Toledo 1085, Cordova 1236, Valencia 1238, and Seville 1248) – their intellectual, scientific and behavioral sciences were taken over by the conquerors just like booty and were, in due course, translated in their own languages. Al-Tunisi (1967, p. 108) quotes Sedillot:[51] 'The Christians who drove the Muslims out of Spain obtained through contacts with them in wars their knowledge, industries and discoveries. The Mongols and the Turks who successively dominated Asia became in the sciences the servants of those they had conquered.'

Louis Baeck (1994, p. 119) has classified three periods of translation from Arabic. First from the early twelfth century to the beginning of the thirteenth century 'in which most important texts written by Arab and Greek scholars were translated into Castilian Catalan and Langue d'Oc.' In the second period 'from these vernacular languages, they were rendered into Latin.' The third period starts from the middle of thirteenth century – 'returned to the double pass: Arabic – Langue d'Oc – Latin.' 'In this process of translation the most important Arabic texts on astronomy, mathematics, medicine, *kalām* and philosophy were transferred to the West' (ibid.).

During those days economic discussions formed part of ethical and philosophical discourses, so economic ideas of the Muslim scholars were also translated and transmitted along with their philosophical works and translations. For example, most of Aristotle's views of economic interest are found in *Politics* and in the *Nicomachean Ethics*. Translation of Ibn Rushd's commentary on these two works became very popular in the West. To quote Grice-Hutchinson (1978, p. 73) again, 'Harman's translation of Averroes's commentary on the *Nicomachean Ethics* enjoyed great success and was never superseded. It has been used in all the editions of Aristotle that are accompanied by Averroes's commentaries, and has remained, almost into modern times one of the main sources of Aristotelian economics.' Charles Burnett (1994, p. 1050) considers it a mark of Ibn Rushd's success that 'a far greater number of his commentaries survived in Latin than in the original Arabic.' The transmission of Muslim scholars' thought was not confined to translation of their works. A number of European students traveled to the seats of learning in Iraq, Syria, Egypt, Morocco, and Andalusia where they learned various sciences from Muslim teachers and on return spread their ideas through their own writings or teaching work in their countries (Sezgin, 1984, p. 128). We shall deal with this question in Chapter 8.

NOTES

1. Many scholars have sorted out economic teachings of the Qur'an and *ahadīth* [the Prophet's Traditions] and presented separate collections. See for example, Mawdudi (1963), Khan (1989) and Kahf (1995).
2. The Companions [*Ṣaḥābah*] refer to the faithfuls who had seen the Prophet (pbuh). Amir b. Wathila al-Kinani Abu Tufayl who died shortly after 100 A.H. is styled the last of the companions (Ibn al-Athir (1989), *Usd al-Ghābah,* Beirut, Dar al-Fikr, Vol. 3, p. 41, Vol. 5, p. 180).

   There are a few researches on economic thought of some companions of the Prophet and their followers based on their economic policies and their reflections on economic matters. For example, *'al Fikr al- Iqtiṣād ī 'ind 'Umar b. al-Khaṭṭāb* [*Economic Thinking of Umar, the Second Caliph*] (d. 23/644) (Qala'ji 1408 H); *Abū Dharr al-Ghifārī wa Ārā'uhū fi'l-Siyāsah wa'l-Iqtiṣād* (Abu Dharr al-Ghifari (d. 32/652) and his views on political and economic issues) (al-Aqtash (1985)), *Ishtirākīyatu Uthmān* [*Socialism of Uthman the Third Caliph*] (Shalbi, 1974). And from among the followers *ʿUmar b. ʿAbd al-ʿAzīz wa Taṣ'ḥiḥātuhu li-Bayt al-Māl* [ʿUmar b. ʿAbd al-ʿAzīz (d.101/720) and his Reforms of the Public Treasury] (al-Burno, 1400 A.H.).
3. Zayd b. Ali Zayn al-Abidin (d. 120/740). Grandson of al-Husayn b. Ali, a number of writings and fragments have survived which go under Zayd's name.
4. Abu Hanifah al-Numan b. Thabit (81–150/700–767). The founder of the Hanafi School of jurisprudence was born in Kufah and died in Baghdad. He himself was a businessman. His opinions on different socio-economic issues reflect pragmatic orientation.
5. Malik b. Anas (94–179/716–795). Founder of the Maliki school of jurisprudence, born and died in Madinah, he gave customary usages of Madinah (*ʿamal ahl al-Madīnah*) great importance in derivation of rules. His work *al-Muwaṭṭā* is the earliest collection of *ḥadīth*.
6. Muhammad b. Idris al-Shafiʿi (150–205/767–820). The author of famous work *Kitāb al-Umm*, he was the architect of systematic Islamic Law. He did not himself found a school of jurisprudence; this was done by his disciples.
7. Ahmad b. Hanbal (164–241/780–855), the originator of the Hanbali school of jurisprudence. He studied in Baghdad and received instructions from the great legal theoritician Imām al-Shafiʿi. He is also the compiler of a large collection of *aḥādīth.*
8. Dr Siddiqi (1982) has presented samples of their economic thinking in his paper 'Recent Works on History of Economic Thought in Islam: A Survey', International Centre for Research in Islamic Economics, pp. 4–18.
9. Abu Abd-Allah Muhammad b. al-Hasan al-Shaybani (132–189/750–805) a colleague of Abu Yusuf and student of Imām Abu Hanifah, also co-founder of Hanafi School of jurisprudence, author of *Kitāb al-Kasb* [*The Book of Earning*] first published from Damascus 1980. Al-Shaybani's work deals with the individual Muslim economic behavior, whereas Abu Yusuf's work is originally addressed to the Caliph.
10. Abu Zakariya Yahya b. Adam al-Qurashi (about 140–203/757–818). He flourished in Kufa, Iraq and died in Fam al-Silh, a town situated on Tigris near Wasit. He was a reliable transmitter of traditions. His *Kitāb al-Kharāj* was first published by Juynboll in 1896. Shemesh published its English translation in 1958, Leiden: E.J. Brill, 2nd edn (1969).

11. Abu Ubayd al-Qasim bin Sallam (157–224/774–838) author of *Kitāb al-Amwāl*, one of the most comprehensive earliest records of the financial system of Islam widely quoted by contemporary writers on the subject. Recently it has been a subject of Ph.D. research by Ugi Suharto at the International Institute of Islamic Thought and Civilization, Kuala Lumpur, Malaysia.
12. Humayd Ibn Zanjawayh (d. 251/893) a disciple of Abu Ubayd. His *Kitāb al-Amwāl* is almost a gloss on the book of Abu Ubayd. It has been edited by Dr Shakir Deib in three volumes and published by the Faisal Centre, Riyadh, 1986.
13. Abu Bakr Abd-Allah b. Muhammad Ibn Abi al-Dunya (208–281/823–891). His work *Iṣlāḥ al-Māl* [*Betterment of Wealth*] came in the early third century Hijrah as a befitting reply to the growing *sufism* as an impact of alien culture to which Muslims came across during expanding Islamic rule and translation work. '*Iṣlāḥ al-Māl*' was first edited and published by Mustafa Muflih al-Qudah (1990), al-Mansurah, Dar al-Wafa.
14. Abu Bakr Harun al-Khallal (d. 311/923). Traditionalist, legal scholar and theologian, little is known of his life. He was an outstanding Hanbalite scholar and author of many important works. He taught at Baghdad in the prestigious mosque of al-Mahdi.
15. Commenting on works of *Kitāb al-Kharāj* Spengler says that they 'reflect Islamic thought about 800 C.E. at which time the influence of Greek thought had not yet made itself felt' (Spengler, 1964, p. 270, n 8).
16. Umar b. al-Khattab (d. 23/644). The second caliph who succeeded the first caliph Abu Bakr. He did many firsts in economic field, such as established the formal *Bayt al-Māl* [Public Treasury], introduced custom duty in Muslim land, initiated *diwān* [register of public revenue], etc.
17. Khalid b. al-Walid (d. 21/642). The famous companion of the Prophet who embraced Islam before the conquest of Makkah. Due to his unprecedented bravery at battle fields he was given the title of 'the Sword of Allah'.
18. Al-Hurmuzan (in Persian, 'Hormizan') (d. 23/644). Persian toparch and general, defender of Ahwaz (Khuzistan) from the end of 16/637 to 21/642 who was taken prisoner by Muslim forces at Tuster and was sent to Madinah. It is said that 'Umar, the second caliph, used to consult him on Persian affairs.
19. Abd al-Malik b. Marwan (26–86/664–705). One of the great caliphs of the Umayyad dynasty, brought up in Madinah and died in Damascus, assumed caliphate after his father's death in 65/685. He was first to mint Islamic *dīnār* [gold coin]. Before him only 'Umar coined *dirham* [silver money]. During his reign the Syrian and Persian *diwāns* were translated into Arabic.
20. Khalid b. Yazid b. Mu'awiyah (48–85/668–704). An Umayyad prince who ordered Egyptian scholars to translate Greek and Coptic works on alchemy, medicine and astronomy into Arabic.
21. Abu'l-Abbas al-Mamun (167–218/783–833). The Abbasid caliph who promoted scientific study and the translation of Greek learning into Arabic. For this purpose he established an academy called *Bayt al-Ḥikmah* [The House of Wisdom]. Greek manuscripts were brought there from Constantinople and other places for translation purposes. It was primarily a research institute with a library, scientific equipment, a translation bureau, and an observatory. Instruction was given in rhetoric, logic, metaphysics and theology, algebra, geometry, trigonometry, physics, biology, medicine and surgery (Artz, 1980, p. 151).
22. 'Many Greek books, such as those of Galen, were saved for the Western World thanks only to Arabic translations.' (Lopez-Baralt, 1994, p. 509). So-called Bryson's Greek original is now lost and survives in Arabic translation (Heffening, 1934, p. 595). The Greek version of the Arabic translation of Ptolemy's *Optics* has yet to be found (Burnett, 1994, p. 1054n).
23. 'The so-called Arabic numbers, without which Europeans would never have been able to develop mathematics, were introduced into the West and the Hindu East by the Arabs' (ibid., pp. 509–10). According to Abulafia (1994, pp. 4–5), the Arabic numerals

were first used in Europe by notaries charged with drawing up commercial contracts for use in the Islamic world.

24. Abu Bakr Yahya b. Umar al-Kinani (213–289/828–901), an Andalusian Malikite jurist. His work *Kitāb Aḥkām al-Sūq* [*A Book on Rules of the Market*] is a collection of his lectures. It is perhaps the first work exclusively dealing with issues related to market problems, price, demand and supply, competition, monopoly, etc.
25. Abu Yaʿla Muhammad bin al-Husayn al-Farra (380–458/990–1066) whose work *al- Aḥkām al-Sulṭānīyah* [*The Rules of Government*], like the one by al-Mawardi (introduced below) has some economic content. The two scholars had the same titles for their work and the contents are also similar except where their respective schools of thought differ (Aby Yala was Hanbali while al-Mawardi was Shafiʿi). It is not known who wrote first and who followed suit.
26. Abu Bakr Muhammad bin Ahmad al-Sarakhsi (d.483/1090). A Hanafi jurist of the fifth/eleventh century who lived and worked in Transoxania developing the juristic tradition of the region. He produced a number of works, the most important being *al-Mabsūṭ* (30 volumes) which is a detailed commentary on *al-Siyar al-Kabīr* by Muhammad al-Shaybani.
27. Ali b. Muhammad al-Mawardi (364–450/974–1058), the son of a rose water merchant in Baghdad, his work *al- Aḥkām al-Sulṭānīyah* [*The Ordinances of Government*], translated by H. Wafa Wahba (1996), Reading, Garnet Publishing Ltd., was commissioned by the Caliph. It contains a wide range of subjects including market supervision, taxation and economic role of the government.
28. Fakhr al-Din al-Razi (544–606/1149–1209). Judge, theologian (*mutakallīm*) and historian. His commentary on the Qur'an, *Mafātīḥ al-Ghayb* is characterized by philosophical expositions. It contains some insights which are of interest to economists.
29. Abu Yusuf Yaʿqub b. Ishaq al-Kindi (Latin: Alkindus) (c. 801–873 C.E.), known as 'the Philosopher of the Arabs', was a philosopher, mathematician, and physician. Al-Kindi was the first Muslim peripatetic philosopher, and is unanimously hailed as the 'father of Arab-Islamic philosophy'. He is best known for his synthesis, adaptation and promotion of Greek and Hellenistic philosophy in the Muslim world.
30. al-Husayn bin Abd-Allah Ibn Sina (Avicenna) (370–428/980–1037). Logic, philosophy and medicine were to be his calling in life. His '*al-Qānūn*' [*The Canon of Medicine*] and *al-Shifā* (healing known in the West as the *Sanatio*) was the basis for teaching medicine in Europe until the seventeenth century.
31. Al-Hasan b. Husayn Ibn al-Haytham (354–430/965–1039) (identified with the Alhazen, Avennathan, Avenetan of Medieval Latin texts). Principal Arab mathematician and the best physicist. Born in Basrah and died in Cairo. He was devoted to mathematics and physics but he also wrote on philosophical and medical subjects.
32. Shaykh Shihab al-Din Abu'l-Futuh Yahya b. Habash al-Suhrawardī (549–587/1154–1191) (Persian pronunciation 'Sohrevardi') was a philosopher, a *sufi* and founder of the Illuminationist philosophy. Also known as al-Suhrawardi al-Maqtul ('The Murdered'), referring to his execution for heresy. He is called as Shaykh Al-Ishraq or 'Master of Illumination'. He was one of the greatest masters and presenters of the philosophy of 'Illumination'.
33. Ibn Tufayl (504–581/1110–1186). Ibn Tufayl was the first Andalusi thinker who knew and used Ibn Sina's *al-Shifā*. The thought of Ibn Tufayl represents a late continuation of the philosophy of Ibn Sina and the more Aristotelian line which would later be represented by Latin scholasticism. Ibn Tufayl's work was not directly known to the medieval Latin scholastics. Translated into Hebrew in 1349 by Moses b. Narbonne, it was edited in 1671 by E. Pococke, accompanied by a Latin version with the title *Philosopus Autodidactus* and met with surprising success in the Western world. His famous work *Ḥayy b. Yaqẓān* (translated by L.E. Goodman in 1972, London) is forerunner of the English *Robinson Crusoe*.
34. Nasir al-Din Abu Jaʿfar al-Tusi (597–672/1201–1274). Born at Tus, Iran and died in Baghdad, began his career as astrologer, later became the trusted adviser to Hulagu

for the conquest of Baghdad in 1258, became vizier and superviser of *waqf* estates and retained his influential position under Abaqa also without interruption until his death. Of economic interest is his treatise on finance – *Risālah Mālīyah*, and *Akhlāq-e-Naṣirī.*

35. The existence of reference to Bryson's name (even now there is no agreement on the exact character of his name, written differently as Brason, Abrussan, Brasson, Brusson (Spengler, 1964, pp. 276, 278, 279, 280, 281, etc.) and Barses, Brasius, Thrasius, etc. (Essid, 1995, p. 182) does not mean that the entire contribution of Muslim scholars in indebted to Bryson, especially when his text teaches nothing new. For more details refer to Islahi (2008[a]), 'The Myth of Bryson and Economic Thought in Islam', *Journal of King Abdulaziz University: Islamic Economics,* **21** (1), 57–64.
36. The idea that 'the bad money drives out good money' known as Gresham's law is a case in point which was mentioned by many scholars like Ibn Taymiyah (d. 1328) Nicole Oresme (d. 1382), etc., much before Thomas Gresham (1519–1579) (Islahi 1988, pp. 139, 143). The idea of division of labor is another case which was explained by al-Ghazali citing the example of a needle, analogous to Adam Smith's famous pin factory example seven centuries later.
37. For instance 'The theory of rent was developed separately by four writers . . . all published during Feb. 1815, Malthus, Edward West, Ricardo and Robert Torrens.' 'This coincidence is an interesting example of how a pressing contemporary issue can call forth a theory developed independently by different people' (Oser and Blanchfield, 1975, pp. 93–4). Again, the 'marginalist school developed in several countries and through the efforts of different people working independently by each other at first . . ., another interesting case of new ideas arising almost simultaneously in different places and from different people' (ibid. p. 220).
38. Harith b. Asad al-Muhasibi (d. 243/857). Born in Basrah and died in Baghdad, a theologian who advocated the use of reason ['*aql*] but finally adopted a life of ascetic renunciation. His principal works are *Riʿāyah li Ḥuqūq-Allāh, Waṣayā, Kitāb al-Tawahhum, al-Rizq al-Ḥalāl.*
39. Al-Junayd b. Muhammad al-Baghdadi (d. 298/910). The celebrated *sufi*, studied law under Abu Thawr (d. 240/854) and associated with Harith al-Muhasibi (d. 243/857). Al-Junayd by his clear perception and absolute self-control laid the foundation on which *sufism* was built.
40. Abd al-Qadir al-Gilani (470–561/1077–1166), the founder of *Qadirīyah* order of *sufism.* He was born in the region of Jilan in the Mazandaran province of Iran, but lived and died in Baghdad. He was a great *ṣūfi*, teacher, preacher and writer. His most famous work is *Futūḥ al-Ghayb* [*Revelations of the Unseen*].
41. Shihab al-Din Abu Hafs Umar b. Muhammad al-Suhrawardi (539–632/1145–1234) is the founder of the famous *ṣūfi* order, '*Suhrawardīyah*'. He was born in Suhraward, a town at that time situated near Zanjan in Iran. He wrote several books on various topics. One of them is *ʿAwārif al-Maʿārif*, which for centuries has been very popular amongst the *sufis*. It has been translated in different languages.
42. Abu'l-Fadl Ja'far b. Ali al-Dimashqi. Lived in Syria during the sixth/twelfth century, according to another estimate during the fifth/eleventh century. His life details are not known. From his work it appears that he was a practicing businessman.
43. 'The Arabs eagerly absorbed all this Greek learning and carried it into every part of their empire. They were soon able to surpass the true heirs of Greek civilization, the Byzantine, so decidedly that by the eleventh century Arabic works on medicine and other subjects were being translated into Byzantine Greek instead of vice versa' (Grice-Hutchinson, 1978, p. 65).
44. To Burnett (1994, p. 1048): 'The absence of any Muslim involvement in the translation is notable. Most of Alfonso's translators were Jews, and those who were not Jews were Christians who sometimes translated the Castilian text into Latin.'
45. Here are a few names of translators from Arabic to Spanish to Latin or directly to Latin: John of Seville, Dominic Gundisalvo, Andrew, Gerard of Cremona, Galippus, Harmann of Garanthia (Grice-Hutchinson, 1978, p. 73).

46. In the days of Muslim intellectual decadence and spread of imitations, philosophers and *mutakallimūn* faded away and it is the traditionalists who kept the candle of knowledge burning throughout these centuries, although the elements of originality and creativity declined.
47. According to Myers (1964, pp. 39, 42–3), al-Ghazali's works were available in Latin even before 1150 C.E., and St Thomas (d. 1274 C.E.), directly or indirectly, benefited from those books in his efforts to refute arguments of the philosophers and sophists against the faith.
48. Abu Nasr Muhammad b. Tarkhan al-Farabi (Alfarabius) (257–339/870–950), a philosopher and a Neo-Platonist and commentator on Aristotle, and a Turk from Transoxania was a prolific writer who produced more than 100 books of varying length on subjects such as linguistics, logic, mathematics, metaphysics, politics, jurisprudence and theology. He integrated the doctrines of Plato and Aristotle as a single point of view. He is called *al-Muʿallim al-Thānī* [The Second Master], Aristotle being the first. Al-Farabi adapted the theories of Plato's *Republic* in his *Risālah fī Ārā' Ahl al-Madīnah al-Fāḍilah*. He assigned to revelation the same role as Plato did to poetry.
49. Ibn Bajjah (Avempace in Latin and Ibn Bayya in Spanish) (462–523/1070–1138). Born in Saragossa and died in Fez in Maghreb, wrote numerous works, 37 of which have survived, among them are his paraphrasic commentaries on various works of Aristotle. He was influenced by al-Farabi on whose ideas he developed his ideal of a utopian society governed by righteous. To Maimonides, Ibn Bajjah was the principal philosophical source next to al-Farabi. Although there were very few Latin translations of Ibn Bajjah, Latin thinkers also made use of his philosophy. St Thomas Aquinas, for example incorporated some of Ibn Bajjah's ideas into his theology, generally conjoined with those of Maimonedes, when he agreed with them (Hernandez, M.C. (1994), 'Islamic Thought in the Iberian Peninsula', p. 788).
50. Abu'l-Walid Muhammad b. Ahmad Ibn Rushd (Averroes) (520–595/1126–1198). As a philosopher he had little influence in the East, and came at the end of the development of philosophy in Islam and perhaps marking its summit. In Europe he became the great authority on Aristotle's philosophy and a school arose around his commentaries on Aristotle known as 'Latin Averroism' and famous for the theory of the 'Unity of the Intellect'. Pribram (1983, p. 33) writes: 'Also important from a methodological point of view was the school of "Latin Averroists", who achieved a dominant position at the University of Padua about the middle of the fifteenth century.' 'Wherever these intellectual movements, especially Averroism and humanism, could get a firm foothold, the soil was soon prepared for freeing economic thought from the fetters of medieval moral theology and for promoting the adoption of a "natural philosophy"' (ibid.).
51. L.A. Sedillot (1808–1887) was a teacher of history, secretary of the *College de France* from 1832 until his death, and long time secretary of the Ecole des Langues Orientales Vivantes. The quotation is translation of a passage from Sedillot's work *Histoire des Arabes* originally published in 1854 at Paris.

3. The Islamic tradition in economic thought (i): theories of value, market and pricing

Muslim scholars, at the least the groups of *mutakallimūn* and *ḥukamā'*, benefited from the Greek translations. But before they got these translations during the third century Hijrah and subsequent period, they had already developed a host of economic ideas and policy concerns. The union of these two elements provided impetus to this branch of knowledge. Not only did they improve and develop the Hellenic thought, but they also introduced some new concepts.

In this and subsequent chapters, we shall make an attempt to trace evolution of economic concepts in the Islamic tradition. In these chapters we shall give prior attention to concepts than any particular contributor or scholar. This is necessary to show the continuity in the economic thought, though it may involve, to some extent, repetition of personalities, as some writers developed only one specific doctrine while the majority presented their views on many issues within the sphere of political economy. In this study we will try to follow a logical order that we normally find in contemporary texts. Occasionally during our discussion and more particularly in Chapter 7 we shall point out some additions made by the Muslim scholars over their Greek predecessors.

3.1 ELEMENTS OF VALUE THEORY AND THE MUSLIM SCHOLARS

The subject of value received increasing importance ever since economics became a science. Adam Smith (1723–1790) presented the labor theory of value but 'confused' it with the cost of production theory of value (Roll, 1974, p. 162). Ricardo (1772–1823) tried to remove Smith's 'inconsistency' but 'could not be free from confusion himself' (ibid., p. 178). Marx (1811–1889) tried to take the Smithian and Ricardian labor theory of value to its logical conclusion by presenting the theory of exploitation (ibid., p. 266) and invited opposition from every corner. The marginalist school emphasized the demand side or a 'theory of value based on utility as an alternative to the classical theory' (ibid., p. 379) against the classical emphasis of supply aspect. The neo-classical economists tried to put an end to this controversy by combining both demand and supply in determination of value (ibid., pp. 401–2).

If this has been the situation in the scientific age of economics, one may justifiably presume absence of any coherent theory of value in the pre-Smithian period. But it is surprising that these elements of value theory and its main building blocks existed long before the builders of the modern economics.

It is interesting to note that development of the value theory in Islamic tradition took an alternative route. As we shall see below, there had been understanding all along that the value is determined by demand and supply. The writers on the subject did not clearly mention explicitly whether value, such determined, would represent the natural value of a commodity or simply temporary market price. But we can easily infer the nature of value from their respective statements.

3.1.1 Value Based on Marginal Utility

The Muslim scholars perceived value based on marginal utility as early as the second/ninth century, though without using the terminology.[1] Ibn Abd al-Salam[2] quotes Imam Shafiʿi as saying: 'A poor man assigns to one dinar much greater value for himself, while a rich man may not consider hundreds of any big value due to his riches' (Ibn Abd al-Salam, 1992, p. 561). Similar opinion was also expressed by al-Juwayni[3] (1400 H., pt 2, p. 920). Al-Shaybani (1986, p. 50) recognized even the idea of 'disutility' as he says, '. . . a person eats for his own utility and there is no utility after being full stomach, rather there could be "disutility".' The subjective nature of utility is best described by Ibn al-Jawzi[4] (1962, p. 302) who says, 'The extent of pleasure from food and drink will depend on how strong is the thirst or hunger. When a thirsty or hungry person reaches to his initial condition (of satiety), after that forcing him to take more of food and drink will be highly painful (of great disutility).' Thus, it is clear that to these scholars value of an object is a subjective thing and depends on its diminishing marginal utility.

It is due to diminishing marginal utility that al-Dimashqi (1977, p. 116) considers it irrational to spend 'too much money on satisfaction of one need and ignoring the other.' He suggests allocation of income in a way akin to equimarginal rule that one finds in modern economic texts.

3.1.2 Cost of Production Theory of Value

Ibn Taymiyah[5] (1963, Vol. 30, p. 87) thinks that 'value is an increment obtained from both labour and capital. So it should be divided among them as an increment resulting from two factors.' From another statement, it appears that he considers value creation due to all factors, land including water, air and raw material, labor and capital (ibid., p. 120; Vol. 29, p. 103). It means his was a cost of production theory of value.

3.1.3 Labor Theory of Value

Ibn Khaldun insists that 'profit is the value realized from labour' (1967, Vol. 2, p. 272). On another occasion he says, '. . . It should be further known that the capital a person earns and acquires, if resulting from a craft, is the value realized from his labour' (ibid., p. 313); 'it has, thus, become clear that gains and profits in their entirety or for most part, are value realized from human labour' (ibid., p. 314). Going through these statements, Baeck (1994, p. 116) has rightly declared that 'the value of each product, according to Ibn Khaldun is equal to the amount of work put into it.'

Although Ibn Khaldun has not used the term exchange value, it is clear that his intention is the same. Implied in his statement is provision of 'use value' as well since labor 'was desired because of the value realized from it in the form of output which men wanted and for the supply of which labour was entirely responsible' (Spengler 1964, p. 299). One may reasonably think that Ibn Khaldun took the theory of value to the point from where classical economists began their journey. However, from some of his statements it appears that he also has a cost of production theory of value.

3.2 MARKET AND PRICE

The first audiences of Islam were traders. They had experience of markets and their related problems. It did not take them much time to analyze and explain their experiments and observations. In a market, the two forces of demand and supply play vital roles and the price provides guidance for undertaking various activities. The Muslim scholars had deep insight in their analysis of market forces.

3.2.1 Demand, Supply and Price

The question of administrative fixation of price arose during the lifetime of the Prophet (peace be upon him), when prices of wheat rose exceptionally high in Madinah and some people requested that he fix the maximum price but he refused to do so (Ibn Taymiyah, 1976, p. 25). The Prophet (pbuh), by prohibition of hoarding and forestalling and with his remark '. . . let Allah provide them with a livelihood through one another,' approved determination of price by free play of market forces – demand and supply. The Muslim scholars were aware of this mechanism. We find a chain of scholars who visualized this. Perhaps the earliest explicit statement on the role of demand and supply in determination of price came from the leading jurist Imam Shafiʿi. Al-Kasani[6] quotes him to have said that 'the value of a commodity changes each time there is change in the price, due to increase or decrease of people's willingness to acquire the commodity (demand) and depending whether it is available in small or large quantity (supply)' (al-Kasani, n.d. Vol. 2, p. 16).

The earliest account of price movement as a result of good or bad harvest (read increase or decrease in the supply of agricultural product) is found in Ibn al-Muqaffaʿ.[7] But his sole concern was to show its likely effect on the fate of the farmers and revenue of the government collected as fixed land tax (Essid, 1995, p. 101, the author refers to Ibn al-Maqaffa's work *Risālah fi'l- Ṣaḥābah*, p. 76). A similar analysis was provided by Abu Yusuf (1392 H., p. 52) who was assigned by Caliph Harun al-Rashid (d. 193/809) to give his opinion about replacing the land tax with a proportional agricultural tax. He wrote, 'There is no definite limit of low or high prices that can be ascertained. It is a matter decided from heaven; the principle is unknown. Low price is not due to abundance of food, nor high price due to scarcity. They are subject to the command and decision of Allah. Sometimes food is plentiful but still very dear and sometimes it is too little but cheap.' This seems to be a denial of the common observation that an increase in supply results in a decrease of price, and a decrease results in an increase. In fact, price does not depend on supply alone – equally important is the force of demand. There may be some other factors also working such as change in money supply, hoarding and hiding goods, etc. Abu Yusuf says that there are 'some other reasons' also which he does not mention 'for the sake of brevity' (ibid.), and because the context was not demanding for an explicit and detailed description of these factors.

Another early expression of the role of demand and supply came from al-Jahiz[8] in his work *al-Tabaṣṣur bi'l-Tijārah* [*The Insight in Commerce*]: 'Everything becomes cheap if its amount increases except knowledge as its value is enhanced when it increases' (al-Jahiz, 1966, pp. 11–12). He refers to it as an example of Indian wisdom (ibid.). Qadi Abd al-Jabbar[9] (1965, Vol. 2 (55)) enumerates some of the demand and supply functions and attributes them to the Almighty Creator as the final cause, and invites a distinction between what changes we see as a result of market forces and what are seen due to manipulation of some people so that intervention may be resorted to prevent them. Al-Juwayni (1950, p. 367) also thinks that the price which is determined as a result of increase and decrease of supply and demand is beyond the control of an individual. It seems he keeps in mind a perfectly competitive market where an individual buyer or seller cannot influence the price. He is a price taker not a price maker.

Al-Juwayni's disciple, al-Ghazali (n.d.[a] Vol. 3, p. 227), provides a detailed discussion of the role and significance of voluntary trading activities and emergence of markets based on demand and supply in determining the price. To him the markets evolve as part of natural process – an expression of self-motivated desire to satisfy mutual economic needs. According to al-Ghazali the 'mutuality of exchange' requires that there should be specialization and division of labor with respect to regions and resources. Trading activities add value to goods by making them available at a suitable place and time. Self-interest of participants in the market leads to creation of profit-motivated middlemen or traders. It is surprising that in spite of so clear a description of market evolution, al-Ghazali does not explicitly discuss the role of demand and supply. However, his awareness of market forces is evident when concerning high food prices, he suggests that the price should be brought down by reducing demand (ibid.).

Another clear, though brief, statement about demand and supply functions we find with al-Dimashqi (1977, pp. 29–30). The price determined by these forces would be median or just price [*al-qīmat al-Mutawassiṭah*]. He gives interesting names to prices higher or lower than the median price (as some contemporary economists have given names to various types of inflation) (ibid., p. 29). He advocates for the maintenance of a stable median price.

A very clear and rather detailed exposition of demand and supply, and the way prices tend to be determined, has been provided by Ibn Taymiyah. While replying to an inquiry he says, 'Rise and fall in prices is not always due to unfair practices [*ẓulm*] of individuals. Sometimes the reason for it is deficiency in production or decline in import of the goods in demand. Thus, if desire (demand) for a good increases while its availability (supply) decreases, its price rises. On the other hand, if availability (supply) of the good increases and the desire (demand) for it decreases, the price comes down. This scarcity or abundance may not be caused by the action of any individuals; it may be due to a cause not involving any unfair trading, but sometimes it may be caused by unfair practices. It is Almighty Allah who creates desires in the hearts of people (the taste)' (Ibn Taymiyah, 1963, Vol. 8, p. 583).

Ibn Taymiyah's statement is a comment of the commonly held view prevalent at the time that an increase in price is the result of manipulation by market players. He argues that there could be market pressures behind the rise and fall of prices, that is, shifts in demand and supply functions. Thus, at a given price, demand increases and supply decreases, leading to a price rise or, conversely, at a given price, supply increases and demand decreases, leading to an ultimate decline of the price. Similarly, depending upon the extent of change in supply and/or demand, the change in price may be large, small or zero. Various such possibilities seem to be implied in his statement. However, the two changes are not necessarily combined, nor do they necessarily occur together. We can experience the same results if, *ceteris paribus*, only one change occurs. In his book *al-Ḥisbah fi'l-Islām*, Ibn Taymiyah (1976, p. 24) describes the two changes separately: 'If people are selling their goods in commonly accepted manner without any foul-play on their part and the price rises in consequence of decrease in commodity or increase in population (leading to rise in demand) then this is due to Allah.' That is, changes in taste which Allah determines. Obviously, he assumes 'other things remaining the same'. An increase in price due to reduction in supply or rise in demand is characterized as an act of Allah to indicate the impersonal nature of the markets. Elsewhere we have discussed how Ibn Taymiyah identified some determinants of demand and supply which can affect the market price – such as intensity and magnitude of demand (in economic jargon, how elastic or inelastic is the demand), relative scarcity or abundance of a good, credit conditions, discount available for cash payments, and costs involved in procurement of the good (Islahi, 1988, pp. 90–3).

Ibn Taymiyah's treatment of pricing mechanism is outstanding among all Muslim thinkers as we do not find such clear and elaborate discussion by others. His disciple Ibn al-Qayyim,[10] a great thinker in his own right, follows his teacher's ideas and reasoning as they are and/or sometimes supplement with his own arguments (Ibn al-Qayyim, 1953, pp. 244–5, 247–8, 253, 254–5, 264). Thus, we need not study his ideas on this topic separately.

Ibn Khaldun introduced many new determinants of supply and demand and their influence on prices. Among the determinants of demand he noted purchasing power of the community at various levels of social development. It also depends on tastes. Accordingly, composition of the goods demanded and the willingness to buy are different at the beginning of the rule of a dynasty and at its advanced stage (Ibn Khaldun, 1967, Vol. 2, pp. 276–8). Supply is affected by production and procurement costs such as cost of rent, wages, duties, taxes on profits, risks attached to storage (ibid., pp. 339–40, 341), profit expectations (ibid., pp. 301–2, 351–2, 367), etc. According to Ibn Khaldun; 'Moderate profits boost trade whereas low profits discourage traders and artisans while high profits decrease demand' (ibid., pp. 340–41). Implied in this statement is the role of prices in the market and their bearing upon the economic activities. In support of his ideas, Ibn Khaldun presents empirical evidences from different countries and provides a blend of applied economics, though he avoids any quantitative analysis.

3.2.2 Imperfections in the Market and Price Control

The Muslim scholars did not discuss pricing mechanism and market functioning as an intellectual exercise or academic discourse. They did – in the quest of justice for market players when price would be abnormally high – formulate a policy and suggest preventive measures or recommend intervention to strike a balance between interests of the buyers and the sellers. We have already noted that the question of price control arose during the Prophet's time, which he rejected. Because of his refusal, many scholars opposed any price control policy and it became a controversial issue in the literature of Islamic jurisprudence (for details, see Islahi, 1988, pp. 94–7). We confine our review to a few representative scholars who presented economic reasoning in their analysis.

While opposing the administrative price fixation, Ibn Qudamah al-Maqdisi[11] (1972, Vol. 4, pp. 44–5) analyses it from an economic perspective and points out the disadvantage of this form of price control. Price fixing will bring about a result exactly the opposite of what it intends, because 'outside traders will not bring their good where they would be forced to sell at a price against their will and local traders who have the stock will try to conceal them.' The net result will be further shortage and deterioration of the situation. 'The needy consumers will demand the goods and having their demand unsatisfied, will bid the price up. The price will thus increase and both parties will suffer.'

According to Ibn Taymiyah (1976, p. 42) the Prophet (pbuh) did not fix the price because the economic factors were against it. It was not a 'general ruling'. He showed that the Prophet himself recommended 'just price' fixation at two other occasions.

The Muslim scholars had the idea of 'price of the equivalent' [*qīmat al-mithl*] or 'just price' [*qīmat al-ʿadl*]. But their concept of 'just price' was not borrowed from the Greek literature. It originated in Islamic tradition itself as the term was used by the Prophet (pbuh) as well as by his two Caliphs, 'Umar (Ibn Hanbal n.d., Vol. 5, p. 327) and Ali[12] (al-Radi, n.d.,

Vol. 3, p. 110, Vol. 5, p. 342). Ibn Taymiyah's interpretation shows that the just price is one which is determined by the competitive market forces (Islahi, 1988, p. 83). He identifies several characteristics of such a market. He insists that it is not unfair on the part of market participants if prices of goods increase due to competitive market forces. And, therefore, there is no reason for state intervention – unless there are market imperfections like cases of monopoly, oligopoly or monopsony (ibid. pp. 99–100).

Much earlier than Ibn Taymiyah, Yahya bin Umar al-Kinani, a strong opponent of price control, supported price fixation by the authority when collusion of market participants or monopolists violates the interest of consumers and inflicts injury on them by charging excessive price (al-Kinani, 1975, pp. 44–5). He is also against price war and cut-throat competition that spoils the market (ibid.).

For administrative price fixation, al-Baji[13] quotes an earlier scholar Ibn Habib[14] who proposes a committee idea for this purpose. According to him the *imām* [authority in charge] should call a meeting of market representatives. Others also should be admitted to the meeting so that they could verify their statements. After negotiation and investigation about their sale and purchase the *imām* should persuade them to a price that can support them as well as not being harsh upon the consumers. Thus, a consensus should be achieved. Price cannot be fixed without consent and agreement of the buyers and sellers. The rationale for it is to arrive at a fair situation both for sellers and buyers. If a price has been imposed without consent of the sellers leaving them no profit, such a price would be corrupt, foodstuffs would be concealed and people's goods would be destroyed (al-Baji, 1332 A.H., Vol. 5, p. 19).

NOTES

1. The Muslim scholars discovered the root of the idea although they were still short of the terminology and the theory, credit for which, no doubt, goes to the nineteenth century Marginalist school. Since diminishing marginal utility is humankind's everyday experience, there would be no surprise if it is found that similar feelings were expressed by some other ancient thinkers. With thanks I would like to add that one of the anonymous referees of this work pointed out that 'Xenophon (427–355 B.C.) held a similar view in his *Hiero* to that expressed by the said Muslim scholars in the medieval period.' He referred to Robert B. Ekelund and R. Herbert's *A History of Economic Theory and Method*, 1990 edition, McGraw-Hill, p. 16. However; I could not get that edition of the book or the original work of Xenophon to see his exact words.
2. Abd al-Aziz b. Abd al-Salam al-Salami al-Dimashqi (577–660/1181–1262). Also known as *Sulṭān al-ʿulamā*, a *Shāfiʿī* jurist and creative thinker, born at Damascus and died in Cairo. Author of several valuable works.
3. Abu al-Ma'ali Abd al-Malik b. Abd-Allah al-Juwayni (419–478/278–1085). Born at Juwayn, a village of Nishapur, Iran, and died there after spending part of his life in Hijaz and Baghdad. He led prayers in the two holy mosques of Islam in Makkah

and Madinah, hence called *Imām al-Ḥaramayn* [Leader of the Two Holy Mosques]. Author of a number of works in *fiqh* and priniciples of jurisprudence. His work *Ghiyāth al-Umam* (or *Ghayathī*) especially contains a lot of economic ideas, frequently quoted by al-Ghazali and Ibn Taymiyah.

4. Abd al-Rahman b. Ali Ibn al-Jawzi (510–697/1126–1200). Jurisconsult, traditionalist, historian and a prolific writer, lived in Baghdad. Some important works are *Talbīs Iblīs, Ṣayd al-Khāṭir, Zād al-Masīr fī ʿIlm al-Tafsīr* and *Dhamm al-Hawā.*
5. Taqi al-Din Ahmad bin Abd al-Halim Ibn Taymiyah (661–728/1263–1328). Most versatile genius, well versed in *Sharʿīyah* sciences, studied Greek ideas but criticized and rejected them and preferred the pattern of *muḥaddithūn* and jurists. His two works *al-Siyāsah al-Sharʿīyah* (English translation by Farrukh Omar, 1966) and *al- Ḥisbah fi'l-Islām* (translated by Muhtar Holland 1980) present his great insight in economic matters. The collection of his *Fatawa* (35 volumes 1380 H.) has a wealth of materials on socio-economic and religions issues. For his contribution to economic thought one may refer to Islahi (1988).
6. ʻAla al-Din Abu Bakr b. Masʿud al-Kasani (d. 587/1189). One of the greatest jurists of the Hanafi School of jurisprudence, born at Kasan in Farghana, Uzbekistan, and died in Aleppo where he taught in the famous Madrasah Halawiyyah. His main work is *Kitāb Badāʾiʿ al-Ṣanāʾiʿ fī Tartīb al-Sharāʾiʿ* which brought him fame and recognition.
7. Abd-Allah b. al-Mubarak Ibn al-Muqaffaʿ (102–139/720–756). Arabic author of Persian origin, one of the first translators into Arabic of literary works of the Indian and Iranian civilizations. Though he died at the age of 36, he left behind a large number of translation and original works like *Kalīlah wa Dimnah, Khudā Nāmah, A'in Nāmah, Tāj Namah*, etc.
8. Amr b. Bahr al-Kinani al-Basri known as al-Jahiz (150–255/770–869). His works are in various fields – literature, grammar, politics, history and general disciplines. His work *al-Tabaṣṣur bi'l-Tijārah* [*Insight in Commerce*] is no doubt the first to exclusively deal with the commercial activities and trading goods. His other work related to the economic field is *Kitāb Taḥsīn al-Amwāl* [*The Book on Improvement of Wealth*].
9. Abd al-Jabbar b. Ahmad al-Hamadhani al-Asadabadi (325–415/936–1023). Muʿtazalite theologian, lived in Baghdad and Rayy. His most important work is *al-Mughnī* some of whose works are lost while others are published.
10. Abu Abd-Allah Muhammad b. Abu Bakr Ibn al-Qayyim (691–751/1292–1350). Born and lived in Damascus, was the most famous pupil of Ibn Taymiyah and co-associate in his struggle of social and religious reform and academic activities, like his teacher he bitterly criticised the philosophers. *Zād al-Maʿād, Iʿlām al-Muwaqqiʿīn, al-Ṭuruq al-Ḥukmīyah* and *ʿUddat al-Ṣābirīn* are some of his important works.
11. Shams al-Din Abd al-Rahman b. Muhammad Ibn Qudamah al-Maqdisi (597–682/1200–1283), the author of *al-Sharḥ al-Kabīr*, was born and lived in Damascus, champion of Hanbali *fiqh*. He was first to be appointed as Hanbali judge in Damascus which he served 12 years before voluntarily retiring.
12. Ali b. Abi Talib (d. 40/660). The cousin and son-in-law of the Prophet (pbuh) and fourth caliph. His political discourses, sermons, letters and wise sayings are found in *Nahj al-Balāghah*, a collection of the fifth/eleventh century by al-Sharif al-Raḍi (n.d.).
13. Abu'l-Walid Sulayman al-Baji (403–474/1012–1081). A Maliki scholar from Andalus, Spain, in 426/1034 he traveled to the East and stayed four years in Makkah, then left for Baghdad where he remained for three years. In the end he returned to Andalus where he was appointed as a judge. His famous work is *al-Muntaqā* – a commentary on *Muwaṭṭā* Imām Malik.
14. Abd al-Malik Ibn Habib al-Salami (184–238/800–852). An Andalusian scholar, expert of Maliki jurisprudence. He is the author of many books such as *Ḥurūb al-Islām, Ṭabqāt al-Fuqahā, al-Wāḍiḥah fi'l-Fiqh, al-Sunan wa'l-Farāʾiḍ*, etc.

4. The Islamic tradition in economic thought (ii): production and distribution

4.1 PRODUCTION

Inspired by the Qur'anic consideration that engaging in lawful economic activities is seeking 'bounty of Allah' (cf. the Qur'an 62:10 and 73:20) and inspired by the Prophet's (peace be upon him) saying that planting a plant is also a good deed (cf. al-Qurashi, 1987. pp. 115–16), the Muslim scholars gave high value to productive activities. al-Shaybani (1986, p. 40) classified productive activities into four categories: services, agriculture, trade and industry. An eighth/fourteenth century scholar, Muhammad b. Abd al-Rahman al-Wasabi,[1] (1982, p. 8) divides basic sources of earning into three categories: agriculture, industry and trade. Depending upon basic needs of the living entities, al-Ghazali (n.d.[a] Vol. 3, p. 225) classified them into five categories: farming (food for people), grazing (food for animals), hunting (including exploration of mineral and forest products), wearing (textiles or clothing) and building and construction (for dwelling). He suggests another classification of industries quite similar to that found in contemporary discussion, that is, primary, secondary and tertiary, which refer to agriculture, manufacturing, and services respectively (ibid., Vol. 1, pp. 12–13; 1964, pp. 328–9). Traditionally, commerce was assigned high value by the Muslim scholars, because, perhaps, it was once the occupation of the Prophet (pbuh) himself and it was the main source of earning in the Arabian Peninsula. With reference to a *ḥadīth*, al-Ghazali says that trade has nine-tenths of livelihood (ibid., Vol. 2, p. 79). Another *ḥadīth* says: 'A righteous honest merchant will be with the Prophets and truthful ones and martyrs (on the Day of Judgement)' (al-Tirmidhi, 1976, Vol. 3, p. 506). Collections of the Prophet's traditions and books of Islamic jurisprudence have several chapters relating to commercial transactions.

But some other scholars have glorified agriculture such as al-Shaybani (1986, p. 41–2), Ibn Abi al-Rabi'[2] (1978, pp. 112, 151–2), Ibn al-Hajj[3] (1972, Vol. 4, p. 4), Najm al-Din al-Razi[4] (Nadvi, 1976, p. 99), etc. They generally put agriculture on top of all economic activities because it is a source of industry and commerce as well. Not only does it satisfy the basic needs of the farmers but also benfits other creatures (al-Wasabi, 1982, p. 89). Ibn Khaldun considers agriculture an important craft (1967, Vol. 2, pp. 356–7) although he accepts that it has been a source of livelihood for the weak and poor Bedouins. '. . . Sedentary people, or people who live in luxury, do not practice it' (ibid., p. 335). In his *Introduction*, he has shed light on some works on the craft of agriculture. 'One of the Greek works is the *Kitāb al-Filāḥah* which is ascribed to Nabataean scholar Abu Bakr b. Ali Ibn Wahshiyah[5] (ibid. Vol. 3, p.151). 'Ibn al-'Awwam[6] presented an abridged edition of the work' (ibid., p. 152). It may be noted that a part of the Greek work on agriculture was related to sorcery. But the Muslim scholars restricted themselves to the part of the book dealing with plantation techniques only. Ibn Khaldun states that 'there are many books on agriculture by recent scholars. They do not go beyond discussion of the planting and treatment of plants, their preservation from things that might harm them or affect their growth and all things connected with them' (ibid.).[7]

One may not find in the writings of Muslim scholars a description of efficiency-oriented different laws of production, but there are many important production related ideas that are necessary for the continuation and optimization of the production function such as linkages in production activities, division of labor and specialization and role of human capital.

4.1.1 Linkages and Interdependence of Industries

Linkage and interdependence of industries were first mentioned by al-Shaybani (1986, p. 75). Al-Ghazali (n.d.[a] Vol. 4, p. 12) makes it clear when he says: '. . . the farmer produces grains, the miller converts it into flour, and the baker prepares bread from the flour.' His recognition of interdependence of economic activities is shown in his statement: '. . . the blacksmith makes the tools for farmer's cultivations and the carpenter manufactures the tools needed by the blacksmith. The same goes for all those who engage in the production of tools and equipments, needed for production of foodstuffs' (ibid.). We find similar ideas in al-Dimashqi (1977, p. 21) when he says: 'Industries are interdependent. The builder needs the carpenter who needs the blacksmith. The ironsmiths need mine workers who need builders.'

4.1.2 Cooperation and Division of Labor

A natural result of linkages and interdependence of industries was need for cooperation and division of labor. Almost all writers on this aspect of economy mentioned these two subjects. (For example, al-Shaybani, 1986, pp. 75–6, al-Ghazali, n.d.[a], Vol. 4, pp. 118–19; al-Asfahani, 1985, pp. 374–5, al Dimashqi, 1977, pp. 20–1, Ibn Taymiyah, 1976, pp. 79, 116, Ibn Khaldun, 1967, Vol. 2, pp. 235–8, 271–2, 286, 329.) We choose al-Ghazali on division of labor and Ibn Khaldun on cooperation, as representative of the group, to show their insights on the issue.

After describing various aspects of production of daily food, al-Ghazali (n.d.[a] Vol. 4, p. 118) says: 'A single loaf of bread takes its final shape with the help of perhaps more than a thousand workers.' He argues further by using the example of a needle. 'Even the small needle becomes useful only after passing through hands of needle-makers about twenty-five times, each time going through a different process' (ibid., p. 119). One can see how close this is to the classical pin-factory example of Adam Smith (1937, pp. 4–5) seven centuries later in making the same arguments.

We find several passages in *Muqaddimah* of Ibn Khaldun (1964, Vol. 1, pp. 89–91; Vol. II, pp. 271–4, 301–2, 316, 336–41) in which he discusses the importance of cooperation and the advantage of division of labor. He maintains that the division of labor is limited to the functioning of the market. Spengler (1964, pp. 295–6) had best summarized Ibn Khaldun's views on the subject when he said: 'Perhaps the most important of the form of cooperation or organization into which men entered was division of labour (by craft or profession rather than by task) which greatly increased output per worker, elevated a community's capacity to produce above that required to supply elemental wants, and gave rise to exchange and commerce in which producers and merchants engaged, with the kind and quantity of what was produced dependent upon the extent of demand and realizable profit.' The passage is self-evident and does not need any elaboration.

4.2 ECONOMICS OF DISTRIBUTION

Distribution is one of the two main economic problems of humankind, the other being production. There have been differences of opinion among the economists about which one is most fundamental.[8] Again, distribution is of two kinds: functional distribution that takes place as a result of the production process; it may be called initial distribution, and personal distribution which means redistribution. In an Islamic system, the latter is much emphasized and a detailed scheme is found in its basic sources. Muslim scholars have also discussed them elaborately. Elsewhere we have given an account of it (Islahi, 1995, pp. 19–35). In the mainstream economics, analysis of functional distribution has been given more importance. We shall therefore confine our discussion to Muslim scholars' perception of functional distribution.

4.2.1 Profit

It may be noted that Muslim scholars excluded interest (a rate charged on capital lent against the time given for use) from the list of rewards for factors. Capital has to come in terms with the entrepreneur as equity participant and share in loss and profit of the enterprise. Thus, one will never find in Islamic tradition a discussion on interest determination.

As far as rewards of other factors are concerned, they leave them to be determined by market forces and their discussions also come along with the price. However, they always emphasize observation of fair practices and due consideration for weaker players. By doing this one must keep in mind that the enormous amount of 'profit' one would gain in the 'market of the Hereafter' (al-Ghazali, n.d.[a], Vol. 2, pp. 75, 76, 84), meaning by it one's salvation. There seems to be awareness among Muslim scholars of 'abnormal profit' when it is said that 'since profit represents an extra worth', it should be sought from those types of goods which are not necessary for people (ibid., p. 73). According to al-Ghazali, given the sellers' benevolence as well as the norms of trading practices and market condition, the profit rate should be around 5 to 10 percent of the price of the goods; 'One who is content with a small profit has many transactions and earns a lot of profit by large volume of sales and thus he is favored' (ibid., p. 80).

Ibn Taymiyah also suggests that entrepreneurs should earn profit in a commonly accepted manner [*al-ribḥ al-maʿrūf*] without destroying their interest and the interest of the consumers' (1976, p. 37). He is against the abnormal rate of profit exploitative [*ghabn fāḥish*] of a situation where people are ignorant of market conditions [*mustarsil*] (1963, Vol. 25, p. 299). Thus, he opposes price discrimination to maximize profit. 'A trader should not charge from an unaware person a profit higher than he charges from others' (ibid., pp. 300, 361). 'A person known to discriminate in this way should be punished and deprived of the right to enter the market' (ibid., pp. 359–60). Similarly exploitation of a needy person [*muḍṭarr*] who is bound to buy the good to fulfill the need (in other words, his demand for the good is perfectly inelastic) is condemned. The seller must charge a profit equivalent to the profit charged from a person not so bound' (ibid.).

Among other things, profits are related to the risk as is clear from various statements of Muslim scholars. Al-Ghazali says: 'They (traders) bear a lot of trouble in seeking profits and take the risks and endanger lives in voyages . . .' (al-Ghazali, n.d.[a], Vol. 4, p. 118). Risk is involved in partnership, trade and traveling (Ibn Taymiyah, 1986, p. 535). 'Trading risk is to buy goods (at a lower price) to sell it (at a higher price) to earn profit' (Ibn al-Qayyim, 1982, Vol. 3, p. 263). Entitlement to profit is tied with the exposure to risk. Ibn Qudamah[9] says: 'A person has the right to share in the profit if he is ready to bear the loss' (1972, Vol. 5, p.141). While dealing with the partnership business, Muslim jurists have extensively written about the costs that will be deducted from the gross revenue to determine the net profit.

4.2.2 Wages

In the Islamic system labor has been considered as a service carrying a market price and therefore in normal conditions it will be left to the free play of market forces to determine the wage. Although the question of paying just and fair wages has been frequently discussed in Islamic thought, Ibn Taymiyah has rather detailed reflection on wages, so for our purpose it will suffice to present his ideas. He uses terms like 'pricing in labour market' [*tasʿīr fi'l-aʿmāl*], 'wage of the equivalent' [*ujrat al-mithl*] analogous to 'pricing in goods market' [*tasʿīr fi'l–amwāl*] and 'price of the equivalent' [*thaman al-mithl*] (Ibn Taymiyah, 1976, p. 34). To avoid any disputes, wages like prices should be fully defined. He says: 'wages and prices, when they are uncertain and indeterminate as is the case when they are not specified, or are not seen, or their kind is not known, there is a case of uncertainty and gambling' (Ibn Taymiyah, 1964, p. 103). It should be noted that during those days, wages as well as prices were sometimes paid in kind. According to Ibn Taymiyah, the 'wage of the equivalent' will be determined by the quoted wage [*musammā*] if such quotation exists, to which the two parties may refer, just as in the case of sale or hire the quoted price [*thaman musammā*] will be held as the 'price of the equivalent' (Ibn Taymiyah, 1963, Vol. 34, p. 72). Again if there is imperfection in the market, the wage of the equivalent will be fixed in the same way as the price of the equivalent. For instance, 'if people are in need of the services of cultivators or of those engaged in textile production or in construction but these are not prepared to give their services, the authorities may in this case fix the wages of the equivalent' (Ibn Taymiyah, 1976, p. 34). He makes it clear that the purpose of this wage control is to prevent the employers and employees from exploitation of each other. 'The just wage will be decided in such a manner that neither employer can reduce the wage of worker from that equitable wage, nor can the worker demand more than that' (ibid., p. 34).

Ibn Khaldun has also something to say about wages. While giving the substance of his thought, Spengler says: 'what increases the money cost of the worker's or merchants' standard of life is or may be reflected in his supply price' (Spengler, 1964, p. 298). At this he comments that 'Ibn Khaldun's statements suggest, however, that it is usually demand rather than supply that fixes the price of the labour which, though it ought at least to furnish the "necessities of life", often fails to do so in villages and hamlets where demand for labour is negligible'.[10]

4.2.3 Rent

Muslim scholars talked more about 'rental' than 'rent' and mostly of juridical nature. Their statement about economic rent is rare and not very clear. Ibn Khaldun reached very close to Ricardo's idea of economic rent in his example how real estate forms an 'unearned income' for his owner but could not strike it to point the element of rent, '. . . their value (that is, real estates and farms') increases, and they assume an importance they did not have before. This is the meaning of "fluctuation in (the real estate market)." The owner of (real estate) now turns out to be one of the wealthiest men in the city. That is not the result of his own effort and business activity, . . .'[11] (Ibn Khaldun, 1967, Vol. 2, p. 284). Similar is the case when he states:

> The Christian pushed the Muslim back to the seacoast and the rugged territory there, where (the soil) is poor for the cultivation of grain and little suited for (the growth of) vegetables. They themselves took possession of the fine soil and the good land. Thus, (the Muslim) had to treat the field and tracts of land, in order to improve the plants and agriculture there. This treatment required expensive labour (products) and materials, such as fertilizer and other things that had to be procured. Thus, their agricultural activities required considerable expenditures. They calculate these expenditures in fixing their prices and thus Spain has become an especially expensive region, ever since the Christians forced (the Muslim) to withdraw to the Muslim–held coastal regions, for reason mentioned (ibid., pp. 278–9).

Implicit in his statement is that the inhabitants of the interior Spain, who had fertile land and good location, also received that high price and thus they earned the differential rent. Had he made it explicit, he could be regarded the forerunner of Ricardo's theory of rent.

NOTES

1. Muhammd b. Abd al-Rahman al-Waṣabi (712–782/1312–1380). Born and lived in Yemen, author of many work on Shariah Sciences. His work *al-Barkah fī faḍl al-Saʿy*

wa'l-Ḥarkah [*Divine Favor in Economic Efforts and Activities*] presents an Islamic view about economic affairs.

2. The facts about the career of Shihab al-Din Ahmad b. Muhammad Ibn-Abi'l-Rabiʿ (218–272/833–885) are still shrouded in obscurity, but his brief treatise entitled *Sulūk al-Mālik fī Tadbīr al-Mamālik* [*Conduct of the Master in the Management of the Kingdom*] places him among the ranks of major Muslim writers who have dealt with the subject of politics and statecraft as a science.
3. Abu Abd-Allah Muhammad b. Muhammad known as Ibn al-Hajj (d. 737/1337). An expert of Maliki jurisprudence, educated in al-Maghrib, Morocco, and later in Cairo. His work *al-Madkhal ilā Tanmiyat al-Aʿmāl* was published in Beirut, 1972. Shawqi Dunya (1998, pp. 121–73) has examined his economic ideas.
4. Najm al-Din Abd-Allah b, Muhammad al-Razi (564–654/1168–1256). Born at Khwarizm in western Central Asia, and died in Baghdad. He spent his life in *taṣawwuf*. His most important work is *Mirṣād al-ʿIbād min al-Mabda' ilā al-Maʿād* [*Observatory of Servants from Here to Hereafter*].
5. Abu Bakr Ahmad b. Ali Ibn Wahshiyah (lived in the fourth/tenth century). Nothing is known about his life, but a number of works are attributed to him. The language and style of the translations which are attributed to Ibn Wahshiyah are not of those of a native user of Arabic. A detailed study of these works would probably show that in them Syriac served a vehicle for Greek, Pahlavi, and Indian scientific and pseudo-scientific ideas.
6. Yahya b. Muhammad Ibn al-Awwam (d. about 580/1185). Andalusian scientist, famous for his work *al-Filāḥah al-Andalūsīyah* [*Andalusian Agriculture*]. It has been translated into French and Spanish. He is author of a few other treatises.
7. In one of his articles Sanchez (1994, pp. 987–99) gave an account of works on agriculture in the Muslim Spain.
8. Adam Smith assigns so much importance to production that he considers it as the main subject of economics. This is clear from the title of his work *An Inquiry into Nature and Causes of the Wealth of Nations*. On the other hand, to Ricardo, 'distribution' should be the subject of economics. He says: 'To determine the law which regulate this distribution is the principal problem in political economy' (Ricardo, *Principles of Political Economy and Taxation*, Everyman Edition, p. 1). In a letter to Malthus (20 October 1820) he writes: 'Political Economy, you think, is an inquiry into the nature and causes of wealth: I think it should rather be called an inquiry into the laws which determine the division of the produce of industry amongst the classes who concur in its formation' (Letters of Ricardo to Malthus, p. 175), quoted by Gray (1967, p. 158).
9. Muwaffaq al-Din Abd-Allah b. Ahmed Ibn Qudamah al-Maqdisi (541–620/1147–1223) Hanbali ascetic, jurisconsult and traditionalist theologian born near Jerusalem and died in Damascus. He is known especially for his work on Hanbali law: *al-Mughnī* and *al-ʿUmdah*.
10. For his remark, Spengler refers to Ibn Khaldun, 1967, Vol. 2, pp. 273–4, 277, 278–9, 293, 314, 334–5.
11. How close is Ibn Khaldun's statement to one of Adam Smith regarding the rent: 'The landlords like all other men love to reap where they never sowed' (Smith, 1937, p. 49).

5. The Islamic tradition in economic thought (iii): money and interest

5.1 MONETARY THOUGHT

5.1.1 Nature and Functions of Money

First of all in Islamic history ‘Umar, the second Caliph, expressed his intention to issue money of camel skins. The context is not known. However, he refrained from doing so when apprehensions were expressed that this would lead to extinction of camels (al-Baladhuri, 1983, p. 456). Ahmad bin Hanbal is reported to have said that if people adopt something as money, it should be acceptable (Ibn Qudamah, 1972, Vol. 4, p. 176). Ibn Battutah[1] (1968, p. 618) noted in his travel account during the eighth/fourteenth century that the Chinese were using paper money for their sale and purchase. But the Muslim scholars did not develop thinking on this line, though they accepted that ‘money is not desired for its own sake’[2] (al-Ghazali, n.d.[a], Vol. 4, pp. 114–15; Ibn Taymiyah 1963, Vol. 29, p. 472; Ibn al-Qayyim, 1955, Vol. 2, p. 137). Several Muslim scholars discussed the nature and functions of money, merits of bimetallic standard and consequences of bad money and debasement of currency.

According to Qudamah bin Ja‘far[3] (1981, p. 434) money has been invented out of human need to exchange goods with each other and specialization in one’s profession. He visualized various difficulties of barter exchange termed by modern economists as non-proportionality of exchangeable objects, indivisibility of goods, absence of a common measure of value, problem of double coincidence of wants, etc. This led to use of a common denominator for their transactions – gold, due to qualities like durability, easy minting and availability in a reasonable quantity. Suitability of gold and silver to work as money has also been emphasized by later scholars, for example, al-Ghazali (n.d.[a], Vol. 4, p. 92), Ibn Khaldun (1967, Vol. 2, pp. 274, 285), etc. To Miskawayh[4] (n.d., p. 110), a Muslim philosopher who always tried to synthesize Aristotle’s views and Islamic teachings on ethics, money measures the value of various goods and services and establishes equality between them which is not possible in direct exchange without the medium of money. He considers gold, in its capacity of money, as 'the standard for all and everything'. It is the best kind of store of value because 'he who sells many things and picks up gold in exchange for the articles and as a substitute for all of them, has done the right thing, since he can get thereby whatever he wishes and whenever he wishes' (Miskawayh, 1964, p. 29).

Problems of barter exchange and function of money as the medium of exchange, unit of account and store of value, have also been discussed both by al-Ghazali (n.d.[a] Vol. 4, pp. 114–15) and al-Dimashqi (1977, p. 21). In particular, we find al-Ghazali's exposition as lucid as a typical contemporary textbook on the subject. Elsewhere we have analyzed it in detail (Islahi, 2001, pp. 2–4).

Without going into discussion of the difficulties with bartering, Ibn Taymiyah mentioned the two important functions of money – measurement of value and medium of exchange, and warned against any damage inflicted upon these functions by debasing money or circulating two different currencies of the same nominal value but unequal intrinsic value. But before we examine his views on this issue, it seems appropriate to note briefly the ideas of two other Muslim philosophers – Ibn Rushd and Jalal al-Din al-Dawani[5] on the subject of money to make the account as comprehensive as possible.

Since Ibn Rushd's original commentary, in Arabic, on Greek philosophers is lost, our information of his views is based on secondary sources.

Ibn Rushd introduced Aristotle's definition of *nomisma* (the Greek word for money) and his concept of money as a common measure 'between separate things, so that equality prevails in business between things where it is difficult to measure equality in existence.' Ibn Rushd, like his many predecessors, reiterates that money is needed because of the difficulty of transacting business in a barter economy. In this way he emphasizes the first and most obvious function of money – the medium of exchange. (Grice-Hutchinson, 1978, p. 70. She quotes Rosenthal, 1965). According to Grice-Hutchinson, 'Averroes's original contribution to theory is very small. Yet he is of importance in the history of economic thought owing to the part he played in the transmission of Greek economics to the Christian West' (ibid., pp. 70–4).

In a comment on al-Dawani's views on money, Spengler (1964, p. 281) observes that he also developed 'the equality maintaining role of money . . . Money in its capacity as unit of account, intermediated as a common denominator between producers of unlike goods and thereby facilitated their inter-exchange . . .'.

By comparing views of three philosophers – Miskawayh, Ibn Rushd and al-Dawani, we find that they strictly based their ideas about money on Greek philosopher Aristotle and almost repeated the same idea. However, other scholars expanded their thinking on the subject much beyond the philosophical ideas to include most of the functions of money and related issues.

5.1.2 Debasement, Inflation and Quantity Theory of Money

The Muslim scholars have been careful about the preservation of standard money as the Prophet forbade them to break the coins except for genuine reasons (Abu Dawud, n.d., Vol. 13, p. 286) such as being defective. Al-Nawawi[6] thought it prerogative of a ruler to mint or issue money (al-Nawawi, n.d., Vol. 6, p. 10). This is but natural because if it were left to individuals, one could hardly be safe from counterfeited and sub-standard pieces of money.

Al-Ghazali dealt with the problems of counterfeiting and debasement which generally took the form of mixing of inferior metals with gold or silver coins, or mutilation of the metallic content or simply 'shaving' or 'shredding' of some of the metals 'It is a great injustice to place counterfeited money in circulation' (al-Ghazali, n.d.[a], Vol. 2, p. 73). 'Circulation of one bad *dirham* is worse than stealing a thousand *dirhams*, for the act of stealing is one sin and it finishes once committed but circulating bad money is bad "innovation" which affects many who use it in transactions' (ibid., pp. 73–4). But coins of mixed metals are acceptable if the issuer is the state (ibid.). It means that he would have allowed 'representative' or 'token' money as used in the modern times. Ibn Taymiyah witnessed the turmoil resulting from debasement practiced by the Mamluk rulers of his time.[7] It seems he had some idea of the relationship between quantity of money, volume of transactions and price level. He suggested that, 'the authority should mint coins (other than gold and silver) according to just value of people's transactions without any injustice to them (Ibn Taymiyah 1963, Vol. 29, p. 469). He advised the ruler not to deal in money by purchasing copper and minting coins and thus doing business with them. He should mint coins of real value without aiming at any profit by so doing (ibid.). He considered it necessary that the intrinsic value of coin should match with its purchasing power in the market so that no one could profit either by melting the coins and selling the metal or by converting metal into coins and putting them into circulation. To mint coins with a face value greater than their intrinsic value and then buy with them people's gold or silver or other valuable commodities would be debasement of currency and result in inflation and counterfeiting. Even the cost of minting coins should not be included in the value of coins, rather, it should be met by the public treasury (ibid.). The aim was to preserve the just and stable value of currency and to avoid the inflationary trend.

Ibn al-Qayyim has further elaborated his teacher's ideas (1955, Vol. 2, p. 134).

We find a more elaborate account of currency debasement and inflation in al-Maqrizi. While stating the unrestricted supply of copper money in place of gold and silver coins in his time, he reiterates: 'During the reign of al-Zahir Barquq (784–801/1382–99), the Ustadar Muhammad b. Ali was entrusted with supervision of the royal treasury. He was greedy for profits and for accumulating wealth. Among his evil deeds was a large increase in the quantities of *fulūs* [copper coins]; he dispatched his men to Europe to import copper and secured the mint for himself in exchange for a sum of money. Under his administration *fulūs* were minted at the Cairo mint. He also opened a mint in Alexandria for striking the *fulūs*. Large quantity of *fulūs* came into circulation and the *fulūs* became the dominant currency. . . . It caused catastrophe that rendered the money useless and made the foodstuffs scarce . . .' (al-Maqrizi, 1994, pp. 71–2, 77–9). Al-Asadi,[8] a contemporary of al-Maqrizi, notes that besides debasement of currency, there could be other causes for general price rise, such as blocking the arrival of grain in transit to the open market, hoarding and hiding grains by sellers and storekeepers, and monopolies enjoyed by certain sections (al-Asadi, 1967, pp. 143–4). He tried to calculate the inflation rate taking the example of bread. In his opinion, if rate of wheat was one *dinār* per *irdabb* (70 kg), one *raṭl* (450g) Egyptian bread would be available for one copper *dirham*. He considered it the 'normal rate'. If wheat was sold at 2 *dīnars* per *irdabb*, the price of one *raṭl* bread would be 2 *dirhams*. He considered it as *ghalā*' [expensiveness].[9] But if the price was below one *dīnar* per *irdabb*, the *rakhā'*, or inexpensiveness, would be at the same rate (ibid., p. 143). Al-Asadi calculated the price rise for the bread. We can speculate that the same would be true for other goods. Had he included a basket of commodities, he would have been considered the first economist to think of measuring the inflation.

5.1.3 Gresham's Law before Thomas Gresham

In addition to inflation and chaos seen as a result of debasement and counterfeiting of currency, Ibn Taymiyah and al-Maqrizi, the two scholars of Mamluk period also saw and analyzed the phenomenon known in the modern economics as Gresham's Law. According to this law where two different money units of the same face value but varying intrinsic value – in term of the purity of metals – are circulated, the bad money drives out the good money. Ibn Taymiyah says: 'If the intrinsic values of coins are different, it will become a source of profit earning for wicked people who will collect the bad coins and exchange them for good money and then they will take them to another country and shift the bad money of that country to this country' (Ibn Taymiyah, 1963, Vol. 29, p. 469). He mentions only the flight of good money abroad and says nothing about its disappearance due to hoarding or melting. Al-Maqrizi (1956, p. 71) notes the other two factors and says that the copper coins have become the 'dominating currency in the country' and the silver coins have disappeared either due to not minting them at all (that is, they are hoarded) or melting them to make out of it ornaments.

5.2 INTEREST – AN ILL USE OF MONEY

According to all religious and philosophical traditions money was invented to serve as a measure, a medium of exchange of goods and services, and to ensure a just measure of values. It was never desired for itself. But the practice of lending money on interest made the money a source of injustice and exploitation. So strict had been the prohibition of interest in Islam, that the question why interest arises and how its rates are determined, became irrelevant to Muslim scholars. They only tried to visualize its ill effects and exploitative nature (cf. Ibn Taymiyah 1963, Vol. 29, pp. 419, 455; al-Razi, 1938, Vol. 5, p. 92). They were also against making a distinction between interest on a consumption loan and interest on a production loan. The imaginary time value of money, in lending and borrowing affairs, is not acceptable in Islam. 'The possibility of the lender investing his money and earning profit is a matter of conjecture; it may or may not materialize. To exact a higher amount over and above the sum lent, on that conjectural basis is a kind of injustice and exploitation' (ibid.).

The provision of profit and loss sharing has been considered by the Muslim scholars as the alternative of interest for running the business. No one is entitled to a guaranteed profit irrespective of the outcome of business. Profit is to be shared with a predetermined ratio, not on a percentage to be earned on the capital supplied. In case of loss, the capital owner bears the capital loss while the working partner bears the loss of his labor, that is, his labor goes 'unrewarded' (Ibn Taymiyah 1963, Vol. 30, pp. 78, 84, 108–9). He is held responsible if cases of 'moral hazard', substatement of profit or negligence on his part are proved (ibid., p. 88). However, some people began taking interest by fraudulent devices that did not come directly under the definition and practice of interest. Ibn Taymiyah has described some of these tricks. For example, *bayʿ al-ʿīnah*, in which A sells an article to B on credit for sum X+*i* which B will pay at a future date; at the same time A buys back the article from B for the sum X which he pays to B in cash; the purpose of the difference, *i*, in the two sums, is obvious –

interest (ibid. Vol. 29, pp. 30, 432, 439). This practice was prevalent also in Medieval Europe under the name of *mohatra* (Schacht, 1936, Vol. 3, p. 1148; Grice-Hutchinson, 1978, p. 48, 48, 59n). If a third party is also involved in this transaction, it is called *tawarruq*. Taqi al-Din al-Subki,[10] a contemporary of Ibn Taymiyah has dealt with this issue in his *fatāwā* in details. In Egypt the word *al-muʿāmalah* was more common for that kind of business (al-Subki, n.d., Vol. 1, p. 327).

5.2.1 *Ribā al-faḍl* and *ribā al-nasī'ah*

A unique contribution of Islam to economic thought is that it envisaged the occurrence of interest in certain cases of barter that involve exchanges unequal by way of quantity or time of delivery, termed as *riba'l-faḍl* and *riba'l-nasī'ah* respectively. Grice-Hutchinson praises Ibn Asim's[11] contribution in dealing with this subject. Prohibition is based on a group of traditions that report the Prophet saying that 'Gold for gold, silver for silver, wheat for wheat, barley for barley, dates for dates and salt for salt be exchanged, like for like, equal for equal and hand to hand; one who demanded extra or paid extra, indulged in *ribā* (Muslim, n.d., Vol. 5, p. 44). The tradition further reports: '. . . When these commodities differ, then sell them as you like (with the difference of quantity) provided that the exchange is hand to hand (that is, the transfer of ownership takes place at once)' (ibid.).

Analyzing prohibition of such exchange, al-Ghazali explains that the reason is that they involve violation of the nature of functions of money (n.d.[a], Vol. 4, pp. 192–3). To Ibn Taymiyah, the prohibition is just a precautionary measure and it is therefore allowed in some cases of necessity (1963, Vol. 29, pp. 25–6, 428, 454). While analyzing evil of interest in *riba'l-faḍl* and *riba'l-nasī'ah*, Ibn al-Qayyim (1955, Vol. 2, p. 138) thinks that it is also aimed at providing facilities of exchange for those who do not usually have money and their exchange is mainly in the form of commodity for commodity.[12] According to Ibn al-Humam[13] (n.d., Vol. 7, p. 7) and al-Zaylaʿī[14] (n.d., Vol. 4, p. 78) in exchange of similar commodities, possession at once is necessary because on-the-spot delivery is always preferable to deferred delivery, and that the deferred price is less valuable than the present one. Thus, the barter sale of these commodities should be hand-to-hand so that equality in exchange is maintained.

To Ibn Rushd, the purpose of this prohibition was to close the door of cheating that existed there in barter exchange of commodities and gold silver bullion and coins in a society which lacked standardization. He observes:

It is clear from the *Sharīʿah* that the purpose of prohibiting *ribā* relates to the possibility of great cheating that exists therein. Justice in transactions lies in approximating equivalence. So, when realizing equivalence between different things was found to be almost impossible, *dīnār* and *dirham* were made to evaluate them, that is, measure them. As between different kind of commodities, I mean those which can neither be weighed nor measured, justice lies in their being proportionate. The ratio of the value of one thing to its kind should be equal to the ratio of the other things to that thing's kind. To give an example: when a man is selling a horse for clothes, justice requires that the ratio of the value of that horse to horses should be same as the ratio of the value of that piece of clothing to clothes. If the value of that horse is fifty, the value of those clothes must also be fifty. Let it be ten pieces of clothing, for example, that would ensure equivalence. So, these commodities have to be unequal in number from one another in just transactions, as one horse is equivalent to ten pieces of clothing in the example (Ibn Rushd, 1988, Vol. 2, p.135).

NOTES

1. Abu Abd-Allah Muhammad Ibn Battutah (704–780/1304–1378). An explorer and traveler known as the 'Arab Marco Polo'. Born in Tangiers (Tanjah) in Morocco, he traveled across several Eastern countries during a period of 24 years. At the end of his travel he returned to his native place and dictated the description of his travel, *Tuḥfat al-Nuẓẓār fī Gharā'ib al-Amṣār wa ʿAjā'ib al-Asfār*.
2. One can see a marked similarity between Muslim scholars' view about money and Crowther's following statement: 'An essential characteristic of money, which sets it apart from all other substances, is that it is not desired for itself. It is, in the fullest sense, a medium or means or mechanism of exchange' (Crowther, 1967, p. 83).
3. Qudamah bin Jaʿfar (250–320/864–932). Converted from Christianity to Islam during the period of caliph al-Muktafi Bi'llah (289–295/902–908) and held the position of finance secretary in the caliphal administration in Baghdad. The title of his work is *Kitāb al-Kharāj wa Ṣināʿat al-Kitābah.* Part of the book was translated in Shemesh *Taxation in Islam Vol. II*, Leiden: E.J. Brill, (1965). The book is a compendium of positive law, marked by the applied aspect.
4. Ahmad b. Muhammad Miskawayh (320–421/932–1030). Philosopher and historian practised the two disciplines with great competence. Translation of his work on history *Tajārib al-Umam* [*Experiences of Nations*] in seven volumes was published in London (1920–21). As a philosopher, Miskawayh is distinguished by the central importance he attached to ethics. His work *Tahdhīb al-Akhlāq* presents Greek, Persian and Arab and Muslim traditions. He had profound impact on al-Ghazali, Nasir al-Din al-Tusi and Jalal al-Din al-Dawani (in Persian, Davani).
5. Muahmmad b. Asʿad Jalal al-Din al-Dawani (830–907/1427–1501). Born at Dawan (in Persian, 'Davan'), a village near Kazirun in the soutwest of the Iranian plateau, and died in Shiraz. He wrote numerous commentaries on well-known works of philosophical and mystical literature in both Arabic and Persian. Of his Persian works the best known is his edition of Nasir al-Din al-Tusi's *Akhlāq-i-Nāṣirī* which was itself a translation of *Kitāb al-Ṭahārah* of Miskawayh, entitled *Lawāmiʿ al-Ishrāq fī Makārim al-Akhlāq* or more briefly *Akhlāq-i-Jalālī*, translated by W.T. Thompson, under the title *Practical Philosophy of the Muhammedan People*, London (1839).
6. Yahya b. Sharaf al-Nawawi (631–676/1233–1277). Born at Nawa in Syria , brought up in Damascus and spent his academic life there and in final days returned to his native place where he died in his father's house. A great scholar of *hadīth* and jurisprudence.

He approached the Mamluk Sultan Zahir Baybars (658–676/1260–1277) to ask him to free people from war taxes. He is the author of *Minhāj al-Ṭālibīn* (Cairo,1296 A.H.) in Shafiʿi *fiqh*, commentry on *Ṣaḥīḥ Muslim* (Cairo, 1283 A.H.) and many other important works.

7. For monetary irregularities and crises during the Mamluk period, see al-Maqrizi, 1994, pp. 66–72; 1956, Vol. 2, pp. 205–6.
8. Muhammad b. Muhammad b. Khalil al-Asadi (lived in the ninth/fifteenth century). Nothing is known about his life except that he was born and died in Syria. He completed his work *'al-Taysīr wa'l-Iʿtibār wa'l-Taḥrīr wa'l-Ikhtibār fī mā yajib min Ḥusn al-Tadbīr wa'l-Taṣarruf wa'l-Ikhtiyār* in 855/1451. The book has been edited by Abd al-Qadir Tulaymat (1967).
9. In modern Arabic, inflation is translated as *tadakhkhum*. In olden days *ghalā'* was used for the general rise of prices.
10. Taqi al-Din Ali ibn Abd al-Kafi al-Subki (673–756/1274–1355) the father of Taj al-Din Abu Nasr Abd al-Wahhab al-Subki (728–771/1328–1370), was one of the most famous scholars and teachers of his time. He was equally renowned as traditionist, jurisconsult, and interpreter of al-Qur'an, theologian, philosopher, logician and grammarian. For many years he was professor at the great schools of learning in Cairo, as al-Mansuriyah, al-Hakkariyah and al-Sayfiyah. In 739 A.H. he was called to Damascus to take the office of head *qādī*, an office which he held for 16 years. Taqi al-Din al-Subki wrote a number of books. He died in Cairo 756 A.H. A collection of his *fatāwā* has been published in two volumes which contains his different economic ideas.
11. Ibn 'Asim, Abu Bakr Muhammad b. Muhammad Ibn 'Asim (760–829/1359–1426). A famous Maliki jurisconsult and man of letters, born and died in Granada. He was chief *Qadī* of Granada, author of many works on *fiqh* and literature.
12. For a detail analysis of Ibn al-Qayyim's view or *riba'l-faḍl* and *riba'l-nasī'ah*, see Islahi, 1984, pp. 11–18.
13. Abd al-Wahid b. Abd al-Hamid known as Ibn al-Humam (790–861/1388–1457). Born in Alexandria and lived in Cairo. He is famous for his commentary known as *Fatḥ al-Qadīr* on the famous Hanafi book *al-Hidāyah.*
14. Uthman b. Ali al-Zaylaʿi (d.743/1342). Belonged to al-Zaylaʿi in Sumalia and in 705/1305 migrated to Cairo. He was an expert on Hanafi jurisprudence. Authored *Sharḥ Kanz al-Daqā'iq* and *Sharḥ ʿala'l-Jāmiʿ al-Kabīr* and some other works. He is different from the author of *Naṣb al-rāyah.*

6. The Islamic tradition in economic thought (iv): state, finance, and development

6.1 ECONOMIC ROLE OF STATE

The Prophet of Islam (peace be upon him) transformed the disintegrated and anarchic people of Arabia into citizens of an organized state. He gave the necessary principles of good governance and educated his immediate followers in establishing an ideal state based on justice, equity, mutual consultation [*shūrā*] and God-consciousness [*taqwā*]. At the same time, he encouraged people to benefit from good experiences of others. Early writings on political and economic themes started in this free environment. The early writers addressed practical problems arising from the fast expanding Islamic state such as the economic role of government, management of conquered lands, administration of public revenue and expenditure, regulation of markets, provision of necessary supplies, improvement of economic condition of the people and development of economy, etc. The Muslim scholars adopted a pragmatic approach. They freely benefited from writings and experience of other people.

6.1.2 Islamic Political Economic Writings v Persian 'Mirrors for Princes'

Islam taught its followers, be it the rulers or the subjects, to be sincere and just towards each other and always encouraged healthy criticism and fruitful counsels. For this reason that we find a chain of writings on statecraft and rules of governance in early writings. Abu Yusuf's *Kitāb al-Kharāj* is an outstanding example of such writings. Some other works are *Daʿā'im al-Islām* by Abu Hanifah al-Nuʿman al-Ismaʿili,[1] *al-Siyāsah* by al-Maghribi,[2] *al-Aḥkām al-Sulṭānīyah* each by Abu Yala al-Farra and al-Mawardi,[3] *Siyāsat Nāmah* by Nizam al-Mulk al-Tusi,[4] *al-Tibr al-Masbūk fi Naṣīḥat al-Mulūk* by al-Ghazali, *Sirāj al-Mulūk* by al-Turtushi,[5] *Qabūs Nāmah* by Kay Kaus,[6] *al-Siyāsah al-Sharʿīyah* by Ibn Taymiyah, *Taḥrīr al-Aḥkām fī Tadbīr Ahl al-Islām* by Ibn Jamaʿah,[7] *Tuḥfat al-Turk* by al-Tarasusi[8] and *al-Sulūk* by al-Mawsili[9] (all in chronological order starting from the second/eighth century to the eighth/fourteenth century). In addition to rules for good governance, these works are a rich source of Islamic political economy.[10]

In the Persian tradition we find examples of such works known by Western writers as 'Mirrors for Princes'[11] and some of them were translated into Arabic during the 'translation phase' in the development of Islamic culture. The Muslim scholars of the later period benefited from these works as is evident from quotations, examples, and episodes reported in some works. However, a wide difference exists between the Persian 'Mirrors for Princes' and other Islamic political writings. For example, in the opinion of a contemporary writer, the 'mirror' gives the image of the king as that of an arrogant despot whom one serves at the risk of one's life and for whom one must show uncritical admiration; 'No mention is made of the ruler's subject, or of justice' (Essid, 1987, p. 23).

Political writings by the Muslim scholars most often emphasize that authority of the ruler is not absolute. They treat it as trust from God. Addressing Caliph Harun al-Rashid, Abu Yusuf (1392, p. 5) said: 'Take care of what Allah has assigned to you and fulfil obligation of authority entrusted to you.' They emphasize maintenance of 'justice'. For example: 'The just government will stay even if its ruler is a non-believer, and the unjust government will decline even its ruler is a Muslim' (Ibn Taymiyah, 1976, p. 94). The literature assigns great importance to economic issues, in particular, supervision of markets, and development of economy and public finance.

6.1.3 Works on *al-Ḥisbah*

In the Islamic tradition a specialized kind of works appeared, known as *al-hisbah* literature, which refers to the 'control function of the government through persons acting especially in the field of morals, religion and economy, and generally in areas of collective or public life, to achieve justice and righteousness according to the principles of Islam and commonly known good customs of time and place' (al-Mubarak, 1973, pp. 73–4). In brief it was office to control market and common morals (Ziadeh, 1963, p. 32).

Most writers dealing with state and economy have chapters or sections on *al-ḥisbah*. However, some writers have exclusively written on this institution. For example, al-Shayzari,[12] Ibn al-Ukhuwwah,[13] Ibn Bassam,[14] al-Jarsifi,[15] Ibn Taymiyah, al-Uqbani,[16] Ibn Abdun,[17] Ibn Abd al-Rauf,[18] al-Saqati,[19] Taj al-Din al-Subki,[20] and Umar b. Muhammad al-Sunnami.[21] These authors either describe virtues and obligations of *muḥtasib* (officer in charge of *al-ḥisbah*) or describe practical and technical details of supervision for guidance to control professions, and product quality and standards. Awwad mentions two works which fall under our study period – *al-Ḥisbah al-Saghīr* and *al-Ḥisbah al-Kabīr* by Abu'l-Abbas Ahmad al-Sarakhsi (d. 286/898) who was himself the *muḥtasib* of Baghdad. Awwad (1943, 18: 420) thinks that these books have not survived and are lost to posterity.[22]

Al-ḥisbah was an important institution of the Islamic state. The government exercised a comprehensive socio-economic control on trade and economic practices through office of the *muḥtasib*. Economic functions of the *muḥtasib* included: ensuring supply and provision of necessities (Ziadeh, 1963, p. 40), supervision of industry (Ibn Taymiyah 1976, p. 21), resolution of industrial disputes (ibid., p. 34), supervision of trading practices, standardization of weight and measures (ibid., pp. 21–2), prevention of injurious economic activities like adulteration (ibid.), check on interception of supply through forestalling, hoarding or coalition of oligopolists (ibid. 23) and fixing of prices, wages and rentals if necessary (ibid., p. 24; Ziadeh, 1963, pp. 54–96). At present, no single office can be compared with the *ḥisbah*. Its multifarious activities are now carried out by different ministries and their special departments. The nearest group of offices are the regulatory agencies which oversee financial markets, trade and commerce and ensure weights, measures and standards.

In Greek and Roman traditions also, activities of market place were administered by the market inspector or *agoranomos* (Lowry, 1987, pp. 238–40). On basis of this partial similarity it has been claimed that the concept of Islamic *ḥisbah* is borrowed from the European *agoranomos*. But the Muslim scholars insist that it owes its origin to the Qur'an itself. For example, al-Mawardi (1973, p. 240) refers to the following verse of the Qur'an to indicate the origin of *al-ḥisbah*:

> And from among you there should be a group of people who invite to goodness, and enjoin right conduct and forbid indecency. Such are they who are successful (The Qur'an 3:104).

Ibn Taymiyah also says that all public offices in Islam are meant to enjoin good and forbid evil, and *al-ḥisbah* is such an office. He gives evidences from practice of the Prophet and his rightly guided caliphs who used to inspect the market (Ibn Taymiyah, 1976, pp. 14, 20).

6.1.4 Economic Role of the State

Islamic manuals for rulers (or mirrors for princes, as the Western writers would like to say) are rich in content and comprehensive in coverage –

ranging from religious guidance, maintenance of law and order, internal and external peace and security, to economic welfare of citizen and protection of their property. For example, Abu Yusuf (1392, p. 129) says: 'The ruler is responsible for welfare of the people and must do everything that is good for them.' He quotes a companion of the Prophet, Abu Musa al-Ash'ari: 'The best of men in authority are those under whom people prosper and worst are those under whom people encounter hardship' (ibid., p. 16).

Al-Mawardi enumerated duties of the ruler *inter alia*, to guard faith, execute and preserve justice, protect life and property, establish peace and security, defend the country, manage financial affairs and to give personal supervision to public affairs (al-Mawardi, 1973, pp. 15–16). Describing the economic and development activities of the state, Nizam al-Mulk al-Tusi (1961, p. 11) says, 'He (the ruler) shall build underground conduits for irrigation of land, shall have canals dug, bridges built over wide rivers, and see the land is cultivated; he shall build fortifications, found new cities, build noble monuments and splendid residences, and shall have caravanserais established on highways.'

Al-Ghazali considers the state as a necessary institution, not only for the proper functioning of economic affairs but also for fulfilling divine social obligations: 'The state and religion are inseparable pillars of an orderly society. The religion is foundation and the ruler, representing the state, is its promulgator and protector; if either of the pillars is weak, the society will crumble' (al-Ghazali, n.d.[a], Vol. 1, p. 17; 1964, p. 59). After citing the example of old Persian rulers, al-Ghazali says: 'The efforts of these kings to develop the world were undertaken because they knew that the greater the prosperity, the longer would be their rule and the more numerous would be their subjects'. They also knew 'that the religion depends on authority, the authority on army and the army on supplies and supplies on prosperity and prosperity on justice' (al-Ghazali, 1964, p. 56).

We have already seen how the state played its vital role in the proper functioning of the market and ensuring healthy economic practices through *al-ḥisbah*. The Muslim scholars included in the state responsibility elimination of poverty, supply of necessities, provision of justice and fair distribution, establishment of peace and security, promotion of human values, and building infrastructure for development of the economy. Elsewhere we have discussed these functions with reference to Ibn Taymiyah (Islahi, 1988, pp. 178–86). It appears from the foregoing that the Muslim scholars considered the state an active player and guardian in carrying out the economic activities.

By the time of Ibn Khaldun (eighth–ninth/fourteenth–fifteenth centuries), we notice a perceptible change in the situation especially in North

Africa. The rulers had lost the spirit of the religion; stability was replaced by anarchy; luxurious style of life did away with the simple living; and to stay in power with all these symbols of decadence, excessive taxes were imposed which discouraged the economic activity (Ibn Khaldun, 1967, pp. 89–90). Arbitrary appropriation of people's property by the government led to slack business activity. Trading houses owned by the rulers weakened the competitive spirit of commoners (ibid., pp. 93–6). Perhaps these were the reasons that Ibn Khaldun became inclined toward *laissez faire* policy. Moreover, he thinks that the Government is not a productive sector. Therefore its intervention in markets would spoil economic activities whether under conditions of prosperity or depression.

6.2 PUBLIC FINANCE

The Muslim economic thinking is distinguished from the earlier economic thought as it pays exclusive attention to public finance. This was but natural as the Islamic territory was expanding, new sources of income were becoming available, new heads of expenditure were emerging and the government was facing new socio-economic challenges. Works on taxation (*Kitāb al-Kharāj*) and public finance (*Kitāb al-Amwāl*) first appeared during second/eighth century but within the next few centuries more than two-dozen treatises were written on these subjects. Shemesh (1967, pp. 3–6) gives a list of 21 works from various sources that were written on taxation during the early centuries of Islam. The works that survived include those by Abu Yusuf, al-Qurashi, Abu Ubayd, Ibn Zanjawayh, al-Dawudi,[23] Ibn Rajab,[24] and portions of Qudamah b. Jaʿfar, and al-Makhzumi.[25] In addition to exclusive works on the subject, issues relating to public finance constituted parts of juristic and political writings.

The basic sources of Islam – the Qur'an and *Sunnah* – prescribed a number of financial provisions, some of these are semi-government revenues while others are exclusively government revenues. In addition to the circumstance that needed such discussion, the implications and application of *Sharʿīyah* financial rules also required such writings. This is, perhaps, the reason we do not find such works of considerable quantity and quality in the mainstream economics before the era of modern economics.[26] It is not possible to examine every aspect of the literature here. We shall, therefore, confine ourselves to taxation, state borrowing and public expenditure.

6.2.1 Taxation

The economy in the period under study was predominantly agricultural. Tithe [*ʿushr*] and land tax [*kharāj*] constituted major sources of public revenue. The system of levy inherited from Persian rulers was 'fixed land tax' [*misāḥah*] which was adopted by the second Caliph 'Umar b. al-Khattab (d. 23/644) after careful assessment of the emerging situation due to military victories of the Muslims (Abu Yusuf, 1392, p. 40). For about 100 years after him, the same pattern continued. It was Muʿawiyah b. Ubayd-Allah,[27] a secretary of Abbasid Caliph al-Mahdi (d.169/786) who first suggested the replacement of fixed land tax by proportional agricultural tax [*muqāsamah*] (Rayes, 1957, pp. 44, 55). Harun al-Rashid (d.193/809), the successor of caliph al-Mahdi, referred the matter to Abu Yusuf who, after a thorough study of taxation system, observed that 'the fixed land tax had lost its relevance' and recommended 'proportional agricultural tax' (Abu-Yusuf, 1392, p. 54). In his opinion, the fixed rate of tax causes hardship if the produce is lower than expected but reduces government revenues if the produce is more than expected (ibid., p. 52). The reason is obvious. He stressed that the proportional tax on the produce of land would be fair and equitable for both parties whether the crops are better or worse than the expected (ibid., pp. 53–4).

According to Abu Yusuf 'rates of poll tax and land tax are not predetermined by *Sharīʿah'*. They are variable subject to 'ability of the tax payer' and 'condition of the land' (ibid., pp. 44, 92). The tax collectors should be 'honest' and deal with the tax-payers fairly (ibid., pp. 80, 114, 120). Maximum economy should be observed in the collection of taxes; in no case should the cost of tax collection exceed the amount of the tax collected (ibid., p. 87). Abu Yusuf opposed tax farming [*qabālah*] as it could lead to injustice and exploitation of the farmers except when it is found convenient for the tax payers and they request it themselves and the ruler also considers the request as fair (ibid., p. 115).

Al-Ghazali also advocates observation of the principle of certainty, benefit and ability to pay as he says: '. . . they (rulers) must demand them only at the proper seasons and times; they must know the usages and fix (burdens) in accordance with capacity and ability (to pay). They must be crane-slayers, not sparrow-slayers at the hunt, that is to say, they must take nothing from the poor . . .; they must keep the hearts of the subjects and officials happy by granting them benefit and satisfying their petition . . .' (al-Ghazali, 1964, p. 112).

Ibn Taymiyah wrote *al-Siyāsah al-Sharʿīyah* at the request of the then-ruler Sultan Nasir Muhammad b. Qalawun (d. 742/1341) as an office manual. The work gives an account of the heads of revenue and expenditure of an Islamic government. His contribution to the theory of public finance is enormous which we have discussed elsewhere in detail (Islahi, 1988, pp. 204–20). However, it would be appropriate to reiterate some points. He sums up all the *Sharīʿah*-permitted sources of public revenue under three heads: *ghanīmah* [spoils of war], *ṣadaqah* [poor due], and *fay'* [booty, land tax, revenue from miscellaneous sources] (Ibn Taymiyah, 1971, p. 45; 1963, Vol. 28, p. 562). He is against tax evasion, especially when the tax is levied collectively on a group or community even if the tax is unfair because if a person evades his share of tax, his share will be payable by others in the group who will have to carry an even greater burden (ibid., Vol. 30, pp. 338–9). He advises the tax authority to be fair in levying taxes even if the tax is illegal. He uses an interesting term 'justice in injustice' *al-ʿadl fi'l-ẓulm*] to express the idea. He gives the reason: 'people might accept it if a thing is wrongfully taken from them (but taken) equally (from everyone). But they do not accept it if some are exempted' (ibid., pp. 340–1). He points out that the main reason behind disorder and chaos in his time is the malpractices in tax levy (ibid., pp. 341–2).

Muslim scholars always argued for low tax rates so that the incentive to work is not killed and payment of taxes is made happily (Abu-Yusuf, 1392, p. 121). The most prominent advocate of low tax rates was Ibn Khaldun. According to him when the government is honest and people friendly, as it happens to be at the beginning of a dynasty, 'taxation yields a large revenue from small assessment. At the end of a dynasty, taxation yields a small revenue from large assessment' (Ibn Khaldun, 1967, Vol. 2, p. 89). In his opinion, 'the strongest incentive for cultural activity is to lower as much as possible the amount of individual imposts levied upon persons capable of undertaking cultural enterprise. In this manner such persons will be psychologically disposed to undertake them, because they can be confident of making a profit from them' (ibid., p. 91). Ibn Khaldun has rightly been considered as the forerunner of 'Laffer's curve 600 years before Laffer' (Lipsey and Steiner, 1981, p. 449). In this regard his ideas are 'comparable with those of supply side economics' (Baeck, 1994, p. 117).

6.2.2 Additional Taxes

The question of imposing taxes over and above what is prescribed by the *Sharīʿah* has been a controversial issue among the Muslim scholars. Those who oppose additional taxes, permit it only in exceptional circumstances such as war-emergencies. Imam al-Nawawi (631–676/1233–1277) refused to give a legal ruling in favor of new taxes unless Sultan Zahir Baybars (658–676/1260–1277), the Mamluk ruler of Egypt and Syria, surrendered all ornaments owned by his family and household to the *bayt al-māl* and desisted from extravagance (al-Suyuti, 1968, Vol. 2, p.105). Those who did not rule out deficiency of resources in normal condition and permit imposition of extra taxes include Ibn Hazm[28] (1347 A.H., Vol. 6, p. 156), al-Juwayni (1981, p. 1560), al-Ghazali (n.d.[c], p. 236), Ibn Taymiyah (1963, Vol. 29, p. 194; Vol. 30, p. 342), and al-Shatibi[29] (n.d.[a], Vol. 2, p. 121).

6.2.3 Public Borrowing

There are instances of borrowing by the Prophet (pbuh) for emergency needs and public purposes. But the early writers on public finance, like Abu Yusuf, Abu Ubayd, etc. are silent on this aspect. The reason may be prosperity and surplus funds in public treasury of their period.

Abu Yala al-Farra (1966, p. 253) and his contemporary al-Mawardi (1979, p. 214) are perhaps first to talk about borrowing by the state. They allow public borrowing only as a last resort and in exceptional cases. The reason, perhaps, was that they were apprehensive of the inability of the government to repay the loan or inclination of the ruler to indulge in extravagance. Perhaps due to the same reason the later writers also allowed borrowing by the ruler only when the income is delayed; in that situation the government can borrow to bridge the gap (al-Juwayni, 1981, p. 276; al-Ghazali, n.d.[c] p. 241; Ibn Jama'ah, 1987, p. 151; al-Shatibi, n.d.[a], Vol. 2, p. 122).

There was no concept of deficit financing or borrowing from the central bank, as one finds, in our own age, because this institution did not exist at that time. However, the Muslim scholars opposed debasement and counterfeiting of currency for meeting the government expenditure (al-Ghazali, n.d.[a] Vol. 2, pp. 73–4, Ibn Taymiyah, 1963, Vol. 29, p. 469; al-Maqrizi, 1994, pp. 67–72) because that practice was similar to present-day deficit financing. During the Mamluk period this was quite common but it invariably caused inflation. Al-Maqrizi (d. 845/1441) attributed all economic crises of his time to this policy.

6.2.4 Public Expenditure

In the mainstream economics, exclusive writing on public finance started very late, and the aspect of public expenditure in particular remained neglected even for a much longer time.[30] Contrary to this, as we have seen in the previous section, in the Islamic tradition writing on public finance constituted the earliest works related to economic problems in which public expenditure occupied a considerable portion. Rules governing disbursement of *zakāh* and *ghanīmah* and their heads of expenditure have been mentioned in the Qur'an itself (8:41, 9:6). There is hardly any difference of opinion on that. The major concern of the Muslim scholars had been the welfare revenue or *amwāl al-maṣāliḥ*, a term used by al-Ghazali (n.d.[a], Vol. 2, p. 166) because the revenue was primarily meant for public welfare [*maṣlaḥah*] (Abu Yusuf, 1392, p. 127; al-Qurashi, 1987, pp. 60–61; Abu Ubayd, 1986, p. 3). The welfare revenues or *amwāl al-maṣāliḥ*, comprise *amwāl al-fay'*, one-fifth of the spoils of war [*ghanīmah*], *kharāj* or land tax and other miscellaneous incomes. The state had a role in the management of the public expenditure for collectively obligatory functions [*farḍ kifāyah*] (al-Mawardi, 1979, p. 215). According to Abu Yusuf development projects for the general benefit should be financed by the public treasury as compared to projects that were beneficial to some specified groups, which should be financed by the groups themselves (Abu Yusuf, 1392, p. 119). The idea is similar to what Musgrave (1987, pp. 7–9) states as social goods of general nature where exclusion is not possible and those goods and services where rival exclusion is possible. Provision of the former will be financed by the state exchequer while the latter by direct charging. Similar rule has been mentioned by al-Farra and al-Mawardi also. They call for distinction between projects whose benefit is common to all and projects whose benefit is limited to individuals only. Expenditure on the first category of projects will be the duty of all citizens (to be financed by the public revenue). In the second case, however, everyone cannot be obliged to pay (al-Farra, 1966, p. 253; al-Mawardi, 1973, p. 214).

Abu Yusuf (1392, p. 102) appears to have suggested the application of cost and benefit analysis for carrying out a project when he says: 'The authorities must cancel the project of digging any canal whose real cost or damage is greater than its benefits.' Establishment of justice, security of state and development of a prosperous society are priority areas of public expenditure suggested by al-Ghazali (1964, pp. 56, 76, 81). He included under the heads of public expenditure items like education, maintenance of general law and order, defense and health care, building of social and economic infrastructure, such as roads, bridges, etc. (al-Ghazali, n.d.[a], Vol. 2, pp. 139–40). Ibn Taymiyah has also mentioned various heads of public expenditure such as necessary government officials (Ibn Taymiyah, 1971, p. 65), maintenance of justice (ibid.), education and training of citizens (Ibn Taymiyah, 1963, Vol. 28, pp. 562–7, Vol. 31, p. 14), public utilities, infrastructure and social goods (ibid., Vol. 28, pp. 562–7). In principle, every project of public welfare should be financed by the public treasury (ibid.). The principle laid down by Ibn Taymiyah regarding choice of priorities is to start from the most important and work in descending order, with preference for productive expenditure over unproductive (ibid., p. 566).

6.3 HOLISTIC APPROACH TO DEVELOPMENT

Economic development has been the prime concern for Muslim scholars. To al-Raghib, al-Asfahani[31] (1985, p. 90), one of the assignments of Almighty God to man is to develop the Earth for better living of human beings and other creatures. But only some scholars have presented a systematic theory of economic development. Those who have done so have adopted a holistic approach in which faith and action, spirit and matter, health and education, peace and security, political power and economic elements are inter-connected. For instance, Abu Yusuf remarks: 'God-consciousness [*taqwā*] and personal character of a ruler leads a people to the right direction and absence of these virtues demolishes the foundation of the state' (Abu Yusuf, 1392 A.H., pp. 3–4). 'Justice causes development of a country and increases the income. Divine favor is linked with justice and disappears with injustice' (ibid., p. 120). Economic development needs availability of infrastructure. In view of the importance of agriculture and trade in his time, Abu Yusuf emphasizes provision of irrigation and transportation facilities (ibid., p. 119). Every effort for development is doomed if the country lacks peace and security. That is why he deals with this issue extensively (ibid., pp. 161–94).

Al-Mawardi, in addition to the role of religion and justice (1929, pp. 3–4, 20), emphasizes proper education as a prerequisite for comprehensive development (al-Mawardi, 1979, pp. 15–46). The overall progress depends on six factors: religion, self-rule, peace and security, property and optimization (ibid., p. 80) 'People will improve their condition only if they are obedient, loving and have sufficient resources from four sectors of the economy: agriculture, animal husbandry, trade and industry' (ibid., pp. 135–8).

At another occasion, al-Mawardi (1981, p. 152) presented an outline of sustainable development of the state and economy. Establishment of the state requires foundations of religion, military power and economic resources. State policy should be based on development of the country, protection of citizens, management of army and administration of revenues. Development of a country requires due attention to both rural and urban areas. He mentions certain criteria, such as crime-free society, necessary industries, means of employment, enough drinking water, pollution-free environment, wide road, planned cities and districts, education, training facilities, etc. (ibid.). It is obvious that most of these factors are considered as necessary for human development even in the present age.

Al-Ghazali assigned so much importance to education and training in socio-economic and human development that he discussed its various aspects in about 100 pages of his famous work *'Iḥyā' 'Ulūm al-Dīn* – even the title of this four-volume work indicates the same.[32] He considers development of the economy as part of socially obligatory duties; if they were not performed life would collapse and human beings would perish (al-Ghazali, n.d.[a], Vol. 2, p. 32). He is not in favor of population as a whole to confine itself to acquisition of a mere subsistence level of living. 'If people stay confined to subsistence level and become weak, death rate will increase; work and industry would come to a halt and the society will perish. The religion will also be destroyed, as life is preparation for the Hereafter' (ibid., p. 108). Like other Muslim scholars he holds the state responsible for establishing justice and ensuring peace and security to promote prosperity and healthy economic development. He cites the example of old Persian kings. 'Efforts of those kings to develop the world were undertaken because they knew that the greater the prosperity, the longer would be their rule and more numerous their subjects. They also knew that the religion depends on the authority, the authority on the army, and the army on the supplies, supplies and prosperity on justice' (al-Ghazali, 1964, p. 56). Various segments of life are interdependent. Sustainable growth is possible when all sectors are developed simultaneously. The Muslim scholars had almost identical views on the question of development. This is due to their common social and political context.

A variant view is found with Ibn Khaldun.[33] His political-economic theory of development is in fact a cyclical model of development. He deals with the processes that recur cyclically during relatively normal phases. He divides them into five stages: (1) conquest and success; (2) stability and self-exalting; (3) economic expansion and enjoyment of fruit of development; (4) contentment and compromise; and (5) extravagance, wastage and decadence. A summarized account of these stages is given below.[34]

Supported and strengthened by group feeling and social cohesion, a new ruling dynasty takes over by suppressing all opposition. 'In this stage the ruler serves model to his people by the manner in which he acquires glory, collects taxes, defends property and provides military protection' (Ibn Khaldun, 1967, Vol. 1, p. 353).

In the second stage 'the ruler gains complete control over his people, claims royal authority all for himself excluding them and prevents them from trying to have a share in it' (ibid.). Thus it is a stage of stabilization and consolidation of forces, strengthening further the group feeling and rewarding his supporters.

The third stage is economic prosperity and enjoyment of the 'fruit of royal authority'. Increasing attention is paid to collection of taxes, administration of public revenue and expenditure. Development of cities, construction of large buildings, increase in allowances of officials and general public attract the attention. 'This stage is last during which the ruler is in complete authority. Throughout this and the previous stages, the rulers are independent in their opinion. They build up their strength and show the way for those after them' (ibid. pp. 354–5).

In the fourth stage, 'the ruler is content with what his predecessors have built; he limits his activities, 'follows closely in their footsteps' (ibid.). He takes no initiative by himself. Expansion in politico–economic power stops and some sort of stagnation starts.

In the fifth stage, the ruler indulges in extravagance, lives an extra-luxurious life, wastes resources accumulated by the previous rulers. Incompetent and unqualified followers are entrusted the most important matters of the state. Idle court men are rewarded, and sincere critics are humiliated and punished. The ruler loses all kind of sympathy and group feeling. At this stage rates of taxes increase, while revenues collected decline. The economy is shattered and the social system is disturbed. The government suffers from incurable problems, which leads to its downfall (ibid.) and takeover by a new ruling dynasty, supported by strong group feeling and social cohesion. Thus, the cycle of development sets in again.

The core concept of Ibn Khaldun's theory of development is *'aṣabīyah* [group feeling, social cohesion][35] which keeps people united behind their leader and solid against enemies. It provides stability and strength to political setup of the country, a pre-condition for development efforts (ibid., p. 284). The difference in the degree of *'aṣabīyah* determines the difference in the size and quality of socio-economic development. Like any other thing, *'aṣabīyah* grows weaker after reaching its highest degree. As a result, degradation and corruption starts in which excessive taxation and luxurious living of the ruler plays an important role.

Social cohesion, group feeling and solidarity are bases for cooperation, which is necessary for building an efficient social organization. It becomes important as the state develops. 'Through cooperation the needs of a number of persons, many times greater than their own number, can be satisfied' (1967, Vol. 2, pp. 271–2).

In Ibn Khaldun's scheme of development, size of population also plays vital role. A large population is able to engage in all sorts of economic activities, causing an increase in goods and services, prosperity and welfare and government revenues (ibid., p. 273). Ibn Khaldun's views about population bear the color of modern demographic theory. Population tends to grow where food is abundant and life is comfortable, though rich diets were less favorable than frugal diets to bodily and natural health (ibid., Vol. I, pp. 351–2, Vol. 2, pp. 274–6). Similarly, 'luxury' and 'prosperity' are initially favorable to population growth, stimulating both natural increase and migration (ibid., Vol. 2, pp. 351–3, Vol. II, pp. 280–1), though in time a luxurious mode of life tends to be unfavorable.[36] At the last stage of civilization, increase in population accompanies famine and death. At this stage people generally withdraw from essential economic activities because of the government's oppressive policies and political disturbances resulting in famine and starvation. The increase in death rate is because of increased pollution and diseases (ibid., pp. 136–7).

The development cycle is also linked to public finance. In the initial stage levies are kept low, conforming to *Sharʿīyah* taxes. This causes an increase in entrepreneurial activities allowing tax base and revenue to grow. With the passage of time, the ruler and officials indulge in luxuries. Moreover, the government expenditure also tends to increase. It then becomes necessary for the government to increase assessment and the tax rates. That creates a disincentive for the businessmen and entrepreneurs leading to decrease in productivity and tax evasion. Again the authority increases taxes and again productivity declines further and thus revenue decreases and a vicious circle starts (ibid., Vol. 2, pp. 89–90).

According to Ibn Khaldun, a ruling dynasty has a life span like individuals which is about 120 years (three times a generation's age, 40 years) (ibid., Vol. 1, p. 343) and once decline sets in a state, it cannot be reversed (ibid., p. 117). In the final stage of a dynasty, sickness and weakness strangles the state and the whole nation in such a way that there remains no point of escape. The city culture turns senile by a self-effecting process of urban luxuries. That breeds laxity of morals and corrupt customs, immorality, wrong-doing, insincerity and trickery for the purpose of making a living in any manner, proper or improper, increases among them. The people develop habits of lying, gambling, cheating, fraud, theft, perjury and usury (ibid., p. 293). The socio-economic and moral decay leads to decline of the old system and allows for the rise of a competing new one.

This cyclical interpretation of history does not mean that the new government is going to start from the same level of economic progress from where the outgoing one had started. Some of the infrastructure developed by the past government would remain available to start economic development from a higher point and cover the distance in a shorter period. From a discussion of Ibn Khaldun's 'politico-economic cycles', Spengler concludes that there is 'a bottom' and 'a ceiling'. Economic activity fluctuates within this 'fairly fixed range rather than about a rising trend' (Spengler 1964, p. 293). In his opinion, 'one might reduce Ibn Khaldun's argument to terms of a model reminiscent of J.R. Hicks's, but without a rising floor and ceiling' (ibid., p. 293, footnote 79).

It would be appropriate to mention here a disciple of Ibn Khaldun, Ibn al-Azraq[37] (1977) who improved and clarified most of the ideas of Ibn Khaldun on stages of development in his work *Badāʾiʿ al-Silk fī Tabāʾiʿ al-Mulk*.

NOTES

1. Abu Hanifah al-Nu'man b. Muhammad al-Isma'ili (d. 363/974). Born at Qayrawan (Kairouan), Tunisia, and brought up there. Originally belonged to Maliki school but converted to Isma'ilism. He died in Egypt where he served as chief justice. His most famous work is *Da'ā'im al-Islām*.
2. al-Husayn b. Ali al-Maghribi (370–418/981–1027), also known as 'al-Wazir al-Maghribi'. It is said that his lineage reached the emperor of Persia (Sasanid). His father was close to Fatimide ruler. At the age of 17 he became a court member of the ruler. He left many works on rules of governance, religion and literature.
3. There are some other books on the subject related to al-Mawardi. For example, *Naṣīḥat al-Mulūk* edited by Khidr Muhammad Khidr (1983), *al-Tuḥfat al-Mulūkīyah fi'l-Adāb al-Siyāsīyah* edited by Fu'ad Abd al-Mun'im (n.d.). Nizam al-Mulk al-Hasan b. Ali al-Tusi (408–485/1018–1092), born at Radkan near Tus, Iran. The celebrated minister of the Saljuq Sultans Alp Arsalan and Malikshah was in all but name a monarch and ruled his empire with great success. Worked for the economic and educational development of the country established famous *Madrasah Niẓāmīyah* of Baghdad and brought a number of reforms to win the hearts of the *'ulamā*, elites and commoners. *Siyāsat Nāmah* written by Nizam al-Mulk al-Tusi is a monarch's primer.
4. Abu Bakr Muhammad b. al-Walid al-Turtushi (451–516/1059–1126), also known as Ibn Randaqah. Born at Tortosa, Spain and died in Cairo to which he migrated at the age of 25. Twenty-two books are attributed to him, of which only nine have survived.
5. Kay Kaus b. Iskander's *Qābūs Nāmah* named after his grandfather Qabus b. *Wushmagir*, was composed in 475/1082 as a guide for his son Gilan Shah. Its English translation as *A Mirror for Princes* was translated by Reuben Levy, London, 1951.
6. Badr al-Din Muhammad b. Ibrahim Ibn Jama'ah (639–733/1241–1333), born in Syria and died in Egypt, had been chief justice of the two countries. His work *Taḥrīr al-Aḥkām* is a comprehensive manual for rulers based on the Qur'an and Sunnah.
7. Ibrahim b. Ali al-Tarasusi (720–758/1320–1357). He was born in Damascus. In 747/1346, he was appointed as *qāḍī* of Egypt which post he held till death. He is the author of 11 books on various topics of religion, biography and *fiqh*. His work *Tuḥfah* which he authored during the reign of Mamlūk sultan Nasir Badr al-Din al-Hasan (first rule 748–752/1347–1351, second rule 755–762/1354–1361), is related to Hanafi school, but it is on the pattern of other books on *al-Siyāsah al-Shar'īyah*.
8. Muhammad b. Muhammad b. Abd al-Karim Ibn al-Mawsili (669–774/1300–1372). Born at Balbak,Lebanon and died at Tripoli. He was a man of literature and jurisprudence, authored many books on various subjects.
9. Fu'ad Abd al-Mun'im who edited al-Mawardi's work *al-Tuḥfat al-Mulūkīyah fi'l-Adāb al-Siyāsīyah* furnishes in his introduction (n.d., pp. 6–16) information about more than 40 treatises on Islamic governance and management of the state. Some notable titles are listed below:

    1. *Siyāsat al-Mulūk* by Abu Dulaf al-Qasim b. Isa b. Idris al-'Ijli (d. 225/840).
    2. *Tuḥfat al-Mulūk* by Ali b. Sahl Rabban al-Tabari (d. after 240/855).
    3. *al-Risālah al-Kubrā fi'l-Siyāsah* by Yaqub b. Ishaq al-Kindi (d. 252/873).
    4. *al-Imāmah wa'l-Siyāsah* and *Kitāb al-Sulṭān* by Ibn Qutaybah (d. 276/885).
    5. *al-Wuzarā'* by al-Sahib b. Abbad (d. 385/898).
    6. *al-Siyāsah* by Ibn al-Tayyib al-Sarakhsi (d. 286/899), a student of al-Kindi.
    7. *Kitāb al-Siyāsah* by al-Husayn b. Ali al-Maghribi (d. 418/1027).
    8. *Luṭf al-Tadbīr fī Tadbīr al-Siyāsah* by Abd-Allah al-Iskafi (d. 421/1030).
    9. *al-Siyāsah wa'l-Ādāb al-Mulkīyah* by Ibn Hamdun (d. 562/1167).
    10. *Tahdhīb al-Riyāsah wa Tartīb al-Siyāsah* by Muahammad b. Hasan al-Qala'i (d. 630/1232).
    11. *al-'Iqd al-Farīd li'l-Malik al-Sa'īd* by Muhammad b. Talhah al-Qurashi (d. 652/1254).

12. *al-Ishārah ila adāb al-Wazārah* by Lisan al-Din Ibn al-Khatib (Ibn al-Jatib in Spanish) (d. 776/1374).

10. It is not known why they call it 'mirror', for which Arabic equivalent is '*mir'āh*' and Persian is '*ā'īnah*'. No Arab writer has used the word *mir'āh* in his title. However, some Persian writers have used the word '*ā'īn*', such as *Ā'īn-Nāmah* by Ibn al-Muqaffaʿ or *Ā'īn-e-Akbarī* by Abu'l-Fadl. Either they have confused the word '*ā'īnah'* [mirror] with '*ā'īn*' [rule, manual, law] or the term has been used because these works, like mirrors, reflect ideas that should be followed by rulers.

    In 1943 Abdullah Mukhlis published an article entitled 'al-Tawālīf-al-Islāmīyah fi'l-ʿUlūm al-Siyāsīyah wa'l–Idārīyah' ['Muslim Works on Political and Administrative Sciences']. It contains a list of more than 100 titles related to what is termed by Western writers as 'Mirrors for Princes' or manuals for governance, while in Islamic tradition such works are generally called as '*al-Siyāsah al-Sharʿīyah*' [polity]. The list covers 14 centuries. Most of the works mentioned in the list are unpublished manuscripts in libraries of Arab countries and Turkey, France, Spain, Vienna, and Germany. A major defect of the list is that, except in a few cases, it does not give bibliographical details of the works. The list is in no way complete or exhaustive.
11. Abd al-Rahman b. Nasr al-Shayzari (d. 589/1193). A Syrian who authored *Nihāyat al-Rutbah fī Ṭalab al-ḥisbah* at the request of Salah al-Din al-Ayyubi. It inspired the later works of Ibn al-Ukhuwwah and Ibn al-Bassam. Al-Shayzari himself was a *muḥtasib* and a judge so his work is rich in presonal experience and local traditions of traders and businessmen.
12. Diya' al-Din Muhammad b. Muhammad b. Ahmad, known as Ibn al-Ukhuwwah (d.729/1329), is the author of a voluminous work on *al-ḥisbah* entitled '*Maʿālim al-Qurbah fī Aḥkām al-ḥisbah.*
13. Muhammad b. Ahmad Ibn Bassam lived in Egypt during the seventh/thirteenth century. He used the text of al-Shayzari as the base for his own work but made some additions. He used even the title of his work *Nihāyat al-Rutbah fī Ṭalab al-ḥisbah.*
14. Umar al-Jarsifi, one of the writers on *al-ḥisbah* from Morocco, personal details are not known, completed his *Risālah fi'l-Ḥisbah* in the late seventh/thirteenth or early eighth/fourteenth century.
15. Muhammad Ahmad b. Qasim al-Uqbani al-Tilimsani (d. 871/1467), belonged to a family of jurists, occupied the position of a judge in al-Maghrib. Although his work – briefly called *Tuḥfah* – does not bear the word *ḥisbah* but it deals with the same subject on the pattern of jurists.
16. Ibn Abdun, Muhammad b. Ahmad, a jurist and *muḥtasib* Spanish author of a treatise on *al-ḥisbah*, spent a large part of his life in Seville in the second half of the fifth/eleventh and the first half of sixth/twelfth centuries. His short treatise is a valuable source on urban economic and social life in the Muslim Spain of that period.
17. Ahmad Ibn Abd al-Ra'uf, an author on *al-ḥisbah* from Andalus of a relatively early period. Very little is known about him. His *Risālah fi'l-Ḥisbah wa'l-Muḥtasib* has 37 chapters and is chiefly Malikite in tenor.
18. Al-Saqati of Malaga (about 500/1100). His work *Kitāb fī Ādāb al-Ḥisbah* has been edited by Levi-Provencal and G.S. Colin, 1931.
19. Taj al-Din Abu Nasr ʿAbd al-Wahhab al-Subki (728–771/1328–1370), author of *Kitāb Muʿīd al-Niʿam wa Mubīd al-Niqam*, belongs to a large family of al-Subkis, whose members during the seventh and eighth century A.H. were known for learning, high positions as *qādīs*, jurisconsultants, professors, preachers, and writers. As the family name al-Subki shows and historical records prove, the family came from the village Subk in lower Egypt. The Arabic text of *Muʿīd al-Niʿam wa Mubīd al-Niqam* [*The Restorer of Favors and the Restrainer of Chastisements*] with an introduction and notes was edited by David W. Myhram, (New York, AMS Press, 1978). Reprint of the 1908 edition published by Luzac, London.
20. ʿUmar b. Muhammad b. ʿAwad al-Sunnami (died during the first quarter of the eighth/

fourteenth century). He belonged to a small town called Sunnam in the Patiala district of the Punjab in India. His work *Niṣāb al-Iḥtisāb* is important as a work on *al-ḥisbah* representing the Islamic East, specially the Hanafi school of thought. The author pays more attention to social and ritual affairs. This shows the dominant local effect on this work. Market and economy constitute a very small portion of the book.

21. In 1943, Awwad published an article entitled 'al-Ḥisbah fī Khazānat al-Kutub al-ʿArabīyah' (works on *al-ḥisbah* in Arabian Libraries), in which he gave a list of 64 titles classified in three categories: (1) past works on *al-ḥisbah*, (2) chapters and sections on *al-ḥisbah* in past writings, and (3) modern writings on *al-ḥisbah*. It gives many new titles which are still in manuscript form; while it missed many known titles. Thus, as the author himself admits it is no way a complete or comprehensive list (Awwad, 1943, 18: 428).
22. Abu Ja'far Ahmad b. Nasr al-Dawudi (d. 401/1012). His *Kitāb al-Amwāl* was studied and critically edited by Najib Abdul Wahhab al-Fili and translated into English as a Ph. D. work from the Exeter University, UK, 1989, in two volumes. Al-Dawudi's work is important as it is the only work on the subject from al-Maghrib. It makes use of earlier, now lost, Malikite and non-Malikite studies on the topic.
23. Abd al-Rahman b. Ahmad Ibn Rajab (736–795/1335–1392). Hanbali traditionalist and jurisconsult, author of several voluminous books. Originally from Baghdad, most of his time was spent in Cairo and Damascus. *Aḥkām al-Kharāj* is his work on the subject.
24. Abu'l-Hasan Ali b. Uthman Al-Makhzumi (d. 685/1384). Little is known about him. The title of his work is *Kitāb al-Minhāj fī 'Ilm Kharāj Miṣr*. Part of the book was published under the title *al-Muntaqā min Kitāb al-Minhāj fī Kharāj Miṣr*, Cairo, Supplement aux Annales, Islamologiques (1986).
25. According to Schumpeter (1997, p. 200), 'public finance especially modern taxation first developed in the course of the fifteenth century in the Italian city republics, Florence in particular, and in German free-towns (*Reichsstadte*).'
26. Abu Ubayd-Allah Muʿawiyah b. Ubayd-Allah (d.170/786). Ibn al-Taqtaqa (660–709/1262–1309) gives an account of his organizational and administrative achievements, culminating in the reform of the *kharāj*. He substituted fixed land tax to a proportional tax on the produce payable in kind.
27. Ibn Hazm (384–445/994–1063). Born in Cordoba, Spain, having an accusingly polemical cast of mind, aggravated by his adherence to the *ẓāhirī* [literalist] juridical school. His written products are extraordinary. From an economic point of view his most important work is *al-Muḥallā* which consists of his juridical ideas.
28. Abu Ishaq Ibrahim b. Musa al-Shatibi (d.790/1388). Born and died at Granada, Spain, a Maliki from Andalus, expert of principles of jurisprudence. In his *fatāwā,* he accepts social change and application of *al-maṣāliḥ al-mursalah* (welfare consideration for which there is no specific text). That was the reason that he allowed certain taxes not mentioned in the *Sharīʿah* but made necessary by the economic difficulties of the Nasirid Kingdom in Granada (628–897/1231–1492).
29. As Dalton puts it: 'English economists as a body have had surprisingly little to say concerning the principle of public expenditure' (1966, p. 139). Earlier, Hunter and Allen (1940, p. 19) have said: 'When the entire amount of literature on public finance is taken into consideration, only a small part of it will be found to deal with public expenditure.'
30. Al-Husayn b. Muhammad al-Raghib al-Asfahani (d. 502/1108). A contemporary of al-Ghazali, famous for his Qur'anic studies, especially an excellent dictionary of the Qur'an, *Mufradāt Alfāẓ al-Qur'ān* and his work on ethics *al-Dharīʿah ilā Makārim al-Sharīʿah* (1985), both are published. Al-Ghazali is said to have always had a copy of *al-Dharī'ah* by him. They exchanged ideas together which is clear from similar discussion and examples used in their works.
31. The title *'Iḥyā' ʿUlūm al-Dīn* [*Revival of Religious Sciences*] is a comprehensive work. Since, in Islamic tradition 'religion' covers every aspect of life, knowledge that guides in those aspects is part of the religious sciences.
32. For Ibn Khaldun's theory of development, which concentrates on the economic aspect

rather than the political one, see Ahmad, Abd al-Rahman Yousri, 2001, pp. 109–17.

33. For details, see Ibn Khaldun, 1967, pp. 353–8. It may be noted that sections on *ʿaṣabīyah* (ibid., Vol. I, pp. 313–30), taxation (ibid., Vol. 2, pp. 89–91), population (ibid., Vol. 2, p. 135), trade (ibid., Vol. 2, p. 93), etc. are only explanation of various stages of Ibn Khaldun's theory of cyclical development.
34. Commenting on Ibn Khaldun's theory of *ʿaṣabīyah*, Timur Kuran says: 'Variants of this idea appear much later in the works of a number of extremely influential thinkers, including Marx and Schumpeter. The idea also forms the basis of Mancur Olson's celebrated *Rise and Decline of Nations* (New Haven, CT:, Yale University Press, 1982) although, I might add, Olson fails to cite Ibn Khaldun among the originators of his thesis' (Kuran, 1987, p. 109).
35. For more information about Ibn Khaldun's theory of population, see Spengler, 1964, p. 297.
36. Muhammad b. Ali al-Gharnati known as Ibn al-Azraq (832–896/1427–1489). Born in Malaqa (Malaga, Spain) and died in al-Quds, Palestine. He served as *qāḍī* at various places. He tried to secure help from Egyptian sultans against the invading forces in Spain, but of no avail.

7. Net addition and impact on economic thinking of medieval Europe

7.1 ADDITION TO AND IMPROVEMENT OVER GREEK IDEAS

We have seen in previous chapters that the Muslim scholars started their intellectual journey equipped with the revealed knowledge. As they had the divine touchstone, they were not hesitant in learning the existing human knowledge. In this perspective several scholars diverted their attention toward the Greek philosophy. However, they did not find answers to all questions of their time in the the Greek philosophy. The Muslim scholars found themselves in a better position to address problems of their time as they had support of the divine knowledge. We have discussed their views on several economic subjects in previous chapters that bespeaks of their mastery on the relevant subjects.

It would be interesting to examine the additions made by the Muslim scholars for improving the Greek economic ideas. But this would require a thorough comparative study of the Greek economics and contribution of the Muslim scholars with reference to their respective original sources. However, the scope of the present work does not allow us to delve into this subject in full length. We shall only make a few remarks on the subject.

First, the Greek economic ideas were confined to a few aspects of life such as, 'wants and their satisfactions', 'economy of self-sufficient households', 'division of labor', 'barter', and 'money'. 'This – presumably the extract from a large literature that has been lost – constitutes the Greek bequest, so far as economic theory is concerned' (Schumpeter, 1997, p. 60). The Muslim scholars did not remain confined to these areas. In addition to the Greek ideas, they discussed market function and pricing mechanism, production and distribution, economic role of the government and public finance, poverty alleviation and economic development, etc.

Muslim scholars did not take to Greek philosophy and economic ideas without critical assessment. Al-Ghazali, for example, criticized the Greek philosophy in his work *Tahāfut al-Falāsifah* [*Incoherence of Philosophers*], although 'he follows Plato in describing how the diverse institutions of mankind . . . are successively established in order to meet man's ever-increasing needs, and develops on Aristotelian lines Plato's brief remark that money was invented as a token of exchange' (Grice-Hutchinson, 1978, p. 66). To Ibn Khaldun 'the virtuous state of the Greek philosopher and *Madīnah fāḍilah* [perfect city] of their Hellenized Muslim disciples, were too far away from the concrete aspirations of humans and offered only an elitist and idealized analysis of social reality' (Baeck, 1994, p. 115).

Both Plato and al-Ghazali discuss 'division of labour'. But Plato's notion is seemingly based on a class system. He does not put emphasis upon 'increase of efficiency that results from division of labour *per se* . . .' (Schumpeter, 1997, p. 56), while al-Ghazali, like Adam Smith, highlights its economic efficiency (see above Chapter 4, section 4.1).

Al-Ghazali, Ibn Khaldun and some other Muslim scholars hold the view that the precious metals have been created to serve as money (see above Chapter 5, section 5.1), an idea of Greek origin (Schumpeter, 1997, p. 62), but Ibn Taymiyah regards it as a matter of convention. He says: 'Gold and silver coins have no natural or *Sharīʿah* specification. They depend on people, their custom and social consensus' (1963, Vol. 19, pp. 250, 251, 248–9), so that any commodity could serve as money. 'Even the coins (token money) in circulation will rule as precious metals in measuring the value of goods' (ibid., Vol. 29, p. 469).

Al–Farabi 'opened new horizons with his comments on works of practical philosophy like the *Republic* of Plato and the *Ethics* of Aristotle' (Baeck, 1994, p. 108). But he wrote in 'the historical context of a multinational commonwealth which was quite different from Plato's Athenian polis' (ibid., p. 109). Ibn Rushd's commentaries on Aristotle were also in the line of al-Farabi's 'effort to remove the Neo-Platonic influences' (ibid., p. 111). In his commentary on Plato's *Republic* 'the Andalusian master proves to be more in sympathy with democratic rule than Plato' (ibid., p. 112). Ibn Rushd's addition to Greek economic ideas will be clearer if one compares Aristotle's Greek text and Ibn Rushd's Latin version of his commentary. One will surely find that 'the Andalusian scholar exposes Aristotle's discourse on ethics rather faithfully, but in a more synthetic way than the original' (ibid.). Ibn Rushd's refinement of Greek ideas is also clear from his reflections 'on the terms of exchange and on money'.[1]

How Muslim scholars made additions to certain Greek works generation after generation would be more clear from the following example elaborated by Essid (1995, p. 44). A collection of Greek letters known as *Sirr al-Asrār* and ascribed to Aristotle was translated in the Umayyad period (41–132/661–750) by Salim Abu'l-ʿAla.[2] Its text was used by an Abbasid writer to produce another version who attributed it to Yahya b.

al-Bitriq (d. 220/835). Later, two adaptations transformed the text into an encyclopedic work and sometimes before 941 C.E. the chapter devoted to physiognomy was transformed by a third adaptation. The final adaptation gave it the form in which it is available now which contains elements found in *'Ikhwān al-Ṣafā.*[3] Al-Turtushi (d. 516/1126) who incorporated a part of this version of *Sirr*, in his mirror book drew upon Greek, Persian and Indian models[4] (Grice-Hutchinson, 1978, p. 67), needless to say including Islamic elements. And to mention a few of them, these elements are: equity and social justice, *'amānah* [trust], *'īthār* [sacrifice], *tazkiyah* [self-purification], ethics and spirituality, prohibition of extravagance and wastage, condemnation of extreme luxury, disapproval of appropriation of property through wrong means, provision of the institutions of *ṣadaqah* [charity], *hibah* [gift], *waqf* [endowment], *waṣīyah* [will], *'āriyah* [lending without any charge], etc. This is the most dominating aspect in economic discussions of the Muslim scholars. An overriding concern in works of the Muslim scholars has been *maṣlaḥah* [social welfare or common good], a concept that encompasses all human affairs, economic and others, and which establishes close links between the individual and the society. The idea has been discussed in more details by al-Ghazali (n.d.[a], Vol. 2, p. 109; n.d.[b], Vol. 1, p. 284), al-Tufi[5] (Khallaf, 1954, pp. 88–150), and al-Shatibi (n.d.[b], Vol. 2, pp. 8–25).

Thus, Muslim scholars' contribution to economic thought presented a fine combination of existing major intellectual heritage and revealed knowledge having elements of positive and normative economics, applied and theoretical consideration, unity of worldly life and the hereafter, matter and spirit and health and soul. The thrust of the work depended on the individual scholar's training and background.

7.2 EARLY MEDIEVAL CHRISTIAN WEST HAD NO BASE FOR ECONOMIC QUESTIONS

It is an accepted historical fact that the 'economic thinking' in Europe started with the scholastic philosophers.[6] Writing in *An Essay on Medieval Economic Teaching* of the West, O'Brien says: 'There is not to be found in the writers of the early Middle Ages, that is to say from the eighth to the thirteenth centuries, a trace of any attention given to what we at present day would designate economic questions' (1920, p. 13). According to Jourdain, as quoted by O'Brien, the greatest lights of theology and philosophy in the Middle Ages such as Alcuin, Rabnas, Mauras, Scotus Erigenus, Hincmar, Gerbert, St Anselm, and Abelard, had not 'a single passage to suggest that any of these authors suspected the pursuit of riches, which they despised, occupied a sufficiently large place in national as well as in individual life, to offer to the philosopher a subject fruitful in reflections and results' (ibid., p. 14). Schumpeter, (1997, pp. 71–2) also mentions names of a few Christian authorities like Lactantius (260–340), Ambrosius (340–397), Chrystomus (347–407) and St Augustine (354–430) and observes that they never went into economic problems, though they did go into the political problems of the Christian state. O'Brien mentions two causes of 'this almost total lack of interest in economic subject'. 'One was the miserable condition of society', 'almost without industry and commerce', the other was the absence of all economic tradition' (O'Brien, 1920, p. 14). Not only had the writing of the ancients, who deal to some extent with the theory of wealth, been destroyed, but the very traces of their teaching had been long forgotten' (ibid., p. 15).

There is another reason. Christianity traditionally discouraged man's engagement in economic enterprise. Trade and commerce, until the Middle Ages, were considered sinful, the urge to earn more was an expression of mere avarice. Gordon writes that, 'As late as the year 1078, a church council at Rome issued a canon which affirmed that it was impossible for either merchants or soldiers to carry on their trades without sin' (Gordon, 1975, p. 172). We find some opinions on economic subjects like 'believers should sell what they have and give it to poor', or, 'They should lend without expecting anything (possibly not even repayment) from it' (Schumpeter, 1997, p. 71). It is self-evident that no economic theory can be built on such idealistic imperatives. Thus, the early Christian scholars did not find any basis or incentive for studying the economic problems. This attitude accounts for 'the great gap' from early Christianity up to the middle of the Middle Ages. Lamenting this situation, Schumpeter writes:

> Whatever our sociological diagnosis of the mundane aspects of early Christianity may be, it is clear that the Christian church did not aim social reform in any sense other than that of moral reform of individual behaviour. At no time even before its victory, which may have roughly dated from Constantine's Edict of Milan (313 C.E.), did the church attempt a frontal attack on the existing social system or any of its more important institutions. It never promised economic paradise, or for that matter any paradise this side of the grave. The how, and why of economic problem were *then* of no interest either to its leaders or to its writers (ibid. p.72).

Having no significant teachings on economic matters in their religious sources, the scholastics heavily depended on newly discovered materials. Starting from almost nothing they expressed considerable opinions on economic issues and heavily deviated from early fathers on various matters of economic interest.[7]

7.3 RISE OF THE SCHOLASTIC ECONOMICS

In the above perspective, it is a bit surprising that by the twelfth and thirteenth century C.E., a revolution came in ideas and the prohibited tree of economics became part and parcel of Christian scholastic discussions. The question arises what were the factors that led to this radical change in thinking and how the scholastics were able to develop a large body of economic thought without almost any precedent. Very few historians of the economic thought have tried to address this question. Even those who dealt with it could not fully substantiate their analysis. The great historian of economic thought, Professor Jacob Viner (1978, p. 48), remarks: 'From the thirteenth century on, after the discovery of Aristotle in the Western world, and especially after the absorption of Aristotelian teaching by Albert the Great and St Thomas Aquinas, Christian moral theology became a tremendous synthesis of biblical teaching, church tradition, Greek philosophy, Roman and Canon Law, and the wisdom and insights of the scholastics themselves.' In this statement 'moral theology' refers to scholasticism, economics was a part of it. One may wonder, what is new or unique in these elements. Bible teachings, church tradition, Roman and Canon Law and even Greek philosophy[8] all existed since long ago.[9] Why could such synthesis not be presented during the Dark Ages? Among the above mentioned elements, if anything was new it was Greek philosophy *with the commentary and exposition by the Muslim scholars*. Schumpeter is more explicit[10] (though he mentions it 'marginally' only) when he says: 'During the twelfth century more complete knowledge of Aristotle's writings filtered slowly into the intellectual world of western Christianity, partly through Semite mediation, Arab and Jewish' (Schumpeter, 1997, p. 87). 'Access to Aristotle's thought immensely facilitated the gigantic task before them, not only in metaphysics, where they had to break new paths, but also in the physical and social sciences, where they had to start from little or nothing' (ibid., p. 88). Arnold and Guillaume (1931, pp. 273–4) emphatically say: 'It can hardly be doubted that Europeans took up the study of Aristotle because their zeal of philosophy had been quickened by contact with Arabian thought.'

Schumpeter is correct when he says: 'I do not assign to the recovery of Aristotle's writings the role of chief cause of thirteenth century development. Such developments are never induced solely by an influence from outside' (1997, p. 88). True, this phenomenon cannot be causally explained by a lucky discovery of a new volume of the Greek philosophy. There must have been other factors that affected the wisdom and insights of the scholastics themselves and induced them to change the traditional Christian outlook towards the realities of life and think the way they thought. Of course this important factor was the contact – negative or positive – on various levels with the Muslim scholars, their work, traders, traveling for education or exploration, war and peace, conquest and defeat. Before we shed more light on these points of contact, it would be worthwhile to show a few examples of economic interest of the Muslim influence on thinking and action of Medieval Europe.

7.4 IMPACT OF THE MUSLIM SCHOLARS ON SCHOLASTIC ECONOMIC IDEAS

We have seen above that in the twelfth century C.E. before rediscovery of Aristotle's writing through Arab mediation, the scholastic scholars had to start on social sciences 'from little or nothing'. Just during that era and in the subsequent period we find in the scholastic writings a number of economic ideas which already existed in the primary sources of Islam or which were inferred by the Muslim scholars long ago. Here are some examples.

While prohibiting *ribā* [usury/interest] the Qur'an at the very outset said that it was unjust [*ẓulm*].[11] But the scholastic scholars perceived it as late as the twelfth century. It was considered a great discovery in the Western circles. O'Brien says: 'Alexander III (d. 1181), having given much attention to the subject of usury, had come to the conclusion that it was a sin against justice. This recognition of the essential injustice of usury marked a turning point in the history of the treatment of the subject, and Alexander III seems entitled to be designated the pioneer of its scientific study' (O'Brien 1920, 175).

Raymond of Penafort (d. 677/1275) considers usury as an act of robbery (Langholm 1987, 132). According to Langholm, in *De bono mortis* of St Ambrose, the following plain statement occurs: 'If someone takes usury, he commits robbery, he shall not live' (Langholm, 1998, p. 59). But for Muslims it was a natural corollary of the Qur'an's ultimatum of war by Allah and His Prophet against the usurer (cf. The Qur'an 2: 279).

The Prophet prohibited selling goods to a needy person taking advantage of his need [translated as *bay' al-muḍṭarr*] (Abu Dawud, n.d., Vol. 3, p. 255). In another tradition, charging an exorbitant price from an ignorant person has been considered usury (al- Bayhaqi, 1999, Vol. 5, p. 541). The purpose of these teachings was to protect the needy from exploitation. Perhaps, similar intention led St Aquinas to liken a needy person who borrows on usury to a buyer in need who has to buy something at an excessive price (Langholm 1998, 77). In the scholastic tradition 'it was strictly forbidden to raise the price on account of the individual need of the buyer' (O'Brien 1920, 120).

According to Viner, 'trade was treated in biblical texts as being peculiarly associated with avarice, riches, and luxury. Here the pagan and biblical traditions had much in common' (Viner, 1978, p. 35). But the scholastics accepted trade as legitimate occupation. In the absence of interest the scholastics and the Muslim scholars approved businesses and trade on the basis of *commenda* or *muḍārabah.* According to Cook (1974, p. 238), 'The beginnings of the *commenda* as an accepted legal category in the Italian mercantile cities may have arisen from an acquaintance with the commercial practice of the Arabs.'

The main characteristic of the partnership is 'risk sharing'. The Islamic rule is *al-ghunm bi'l-ghurm wa'l-ribḥ bi'l-ḍamān*, which means a gain is associated with (the agreeing to bear) the loss, and profit entitlement is tied to (bearing of) the risk (al-Sindi, 1986, Vol. 7, p. 255).[12] The scholastic scholars also accepted this rule. According to Baldus (d. 1400), when there is no sharing of risk, there is no partnership (O'Brien 1920, p. 208). It is worthwhile to note that in the medieval period sometimes Muslims and Christians carried such enterprises jointly. Kramers states there were 'many fold ways in which commercial relations led to close cooperation between Muslims and Christians – e.g. in the form of joint partnership and of commercial treaties' (Kramers, 1965, p. 103).

As regards the appropriation of land, the Islamic position is that a person who revives a piece of land (that is, makes it cultivable) is entitled to its ownership (Abu-Yusuf, 1392 H., p. 70–1). This is based on the Prophet's (peace be upon him) saying: 'One who revives a piece of land has right to own it' (al-Tirmidhi, 1976, Vol. 3, pp. 653, 655). In light of this tradition al-Shirazi[13] regards revival of the dead land as a praise-worthy act (1976, Vol. 1, p. 553). The issue has been discussed by the Muslim scholars in almost every book on land management and taxation. St Aquinas also held that 'the expenditure of labour in cultivating an area of land, or occupation of it, can give rise to a just claim of ownership' (Gordon, 1975, p. 182).

The Qur'anic term for surplus is '*al-ʿafw*'. It says: 'They ask thee (O Prophet) how much they are to spend [in the cause of Allah]. Say: '*al-ʿafw*' (Qur'an, 2: 219).[14] The scholastics also recommended alms giving from surplus resources. Viner (1978, p. 73) quotes Thomas Aquinas saying that:

> Alms giving is a matter of precept, but the precept requires alms to be given only out of 'surplus,' or 'superfluity'. . . . 'Surplus' is explained as what the donor does not need for the time being, 'as far as he can judge with probability,' or 'according as things probably and generally occur.' . . . To give as alms what is needed 'if one's life or the life of those under our charge would endanger,' is 'altogether wrong'.

Long ago al-Ghazali mentioned similar views. He condemns a person who has a small amount to support his family but instead of spending upon them he provides a feast to others (al-Ghazali, n.d.[a], Vol. 2, p. 341). He quotes many verses from the Qur'an to support his views: 'Make not thy hand tied (like a niggard's) to thy neck, nor stretch it forth to its utmost reach, so that thou become blameworthy and destitute' (The Qur'an 17: 29). Further, '. . . and squander not (your wealth) in the manner of a spendthrift. Verily spendthrifts are brothers of the evil ones and the evil one is ungrateful to his Lord' (ibid. 17: 26–7). And, 'those who when they spend are not extravagant and not niggardly, but hold a just (balance) between these extremes' (ibid. 25: 67).

In the Middle Ages, the traditional Christian view about private property, then widely accepted, ascribed its origin to human sin. Tawney (1938, p. 45) remarks about Christian ideology: 'To seek more is not enterprise, but avarice, and avarice is a deadly sin.' The ideal community was one in which no one called anything his own, but they had all things common. After rediscovery of Aristotle by Medieval Europe through Jewish scholars and Arab commentators, the concept of private property underwent a drastic change. Aquinas was the first to combine a defense of the Aristotelian view with a full discussion and criticism of the traditional texts (Aquinas, 1947, II. Q. 2, LXVI, art. 2). Private ownership of resources coupled with communal use of surplus produce is Aquinas' program for maximization of total social product and the optimization of its distribution from the viewpoint of economic welfare. Private ownership is advocated mainly on the ground of higher economic efficiency, while the policy of communal use of property derives from moral imperatives; thus Aquinas writes: 'Feed him that is perishing of hunger; if you fail to do so you are guilty of his death' (ibid., II. Q. 2, XXXII, art. 5).

The Muslim scholars took the institution of private property for granted to fulfill certain obligations. Those who are deprived have a share in the property of the rich. Praising the obedient servants the Qur'an (70: 24–5) says: 'And those in whose wealth there is a known right, for the beggar who asks, and for the unlucky who has lost his property and wealth, (and his means of living has been straitened).' Thus, one would not find in works of Muslim scholars any of the arguments which Aristotle has brought against Plato's communism. They believe in sharing of 'have-nots' in the property of 'haves'. But they differ about the nature and extent of sharing. For example, Ibn Taymiyah recommends different punishments for a person who denies an obligation in spite of having means to fulfill it (Ibn Taymiyah, 1963, Vol. 30, pp. 37–9). According to him 'it is people's duty to help others in meeting their need for bread, clothing, and shelter. If they refrain from doing so, the state will step in to compel them to do so' (ibid.,

Vol. 29, p. 194). If a person has goods, and refuses to lend to others who are in need, and as a result the needy person dies, the wealthy person will be held responsible for that death (ibid., Vol. 29, p. 191). We have noted above similar opinion by St Thomas Aquinas. His ideas in this respect seem to be a synthesis of Greek and Muslim views on property rights.

Forestalling (that is, buying from a merchant en route to the market) and town guilds of manufactures and tradesmen attracted attention of the scholastic scholars during the fifteenth century (Gordon, 1975, pp. 219–20). In the Islamic sources we read condemnation of hoarding and prohibition of forestalling known as *iḥtikār* and *talaqqī al-jalab* respectively. The Prophet (pbuh) said: 'The hoarder is committing a wrongdoing and one who brings supply is favoured by livelihood' (al-Sanaʿani, 1403 H., Vol. 8, p. 204; Abu Dawud, n.d. Vol. 3, p. 281). The question of guild's monopolization was discussed in detail by Ibn Taymiyah (Islahi, 1988, pp. 100–2).

Peter Olivi (d. 1298), author of a much-copied treatise on economic contracts opposed price control even when there was general scarcity. He states openly that unless one does this, those holding stocks will be less inclined to part with them, to the detriment of all those who need them (Langholm, 1987, p. 117). Prior to Olivi, Ibn Qudamah al-Maqdisi, in addition to support his stand against the price control with the tradition of the Prophet, says that it is obvious that price fixing must lead to dearth and further rise in the prices. This is so because when the outside traders hear about price control they restrain from bringing their goods to market where they would be forced to sell at a lower price against their will. And the local traders who have stocks will also try to conceal theirs. The needy consumers will demand goods and not finding them easily would be willing to pay a higher price, thus pushing the price level further up. As a result both the buyers and sellers will suffer. The sellers will suffer as they have unsold stocks and the buyers will suffer as their wants are unfulfilled (al-Maqdisi, Ibn Qudamah, 1972, Vol. 4, pp. 44–5).

The aim of the present writer is not to search for all such scholastic economic ideas which have similarity with the ideas of the Muslim scholars. We presented a few samples to establish the fact that the Muslim scholars' influence cannot be ruled out in the development of scholastic ideas which existed in the Islamic primary sources. Some effort would show similarity not only in thought but also in contents of many scholastic works with the Muslim scholars.[15]

The Muslim influence in the Medieval West is also manifest from nomenclature of some economic institutions and business practices whose origin is Arabic, such as *ḥisbah* [agoranomos], mathessep [*muḥtasib*] existed in the Roman East, (Ziadeh, 1963, p. 39; Islahi, 1988, pp. 187–8), *muḍārabah* [commenda], *suftaja* and *ḥawālah, fundaq, mauna* [maona], *ṣakk* [cheque], *tarīf* [tariff], *rizq* [risk], *makhzan* [magazine], etc. Kramers (1965, p. 105) admits: '. . . our commercial vocabulary itself has preserved some very eloquent proofs of the fact that there was a time when Islamic trade and trade customs exercised a deep influence on the commercial development in Christian countries.' 'One of these trade forms was also the feigned bargain called '*muhātra*', which word has also passed from Arabic into European languages' (ibid.). Lopez-Baralt (1994, p. 519) gives a list of several 'Spanish words directly "naturalized" from Arabic, vividly demonstrating the influence of the Muslim civilization on so many aspects of Spanish – and by extension, Latin-American – life and on English lexicon. Most of these words constituted trade items.'[16]

Perhaps the greatest influence of Muslims on Medieval Europe that appeared in the form of change in outlook of the scholastic scholars and European entrepreneurs was toward commerce and trade. Trading was a manifestation of this influence as well as one of the channels through with economic ideas of the Muslim scholars reached the West.

Aristotle equated trade with war. 'Prosperity gained through trade is like the fruits gathered from war and conquest' (Gordon, 1975, p. 41). The Christian tradition also discouraged engagement in trading activities. With this background, how and why a movement of trading activities – mercantilism – emerged in Europe may be a relevant question.

7.4.1 Mercantilism: A Reaction against the Muslim Power

There is no difference of opinion that mercantilism was a dominant current of economic thought during two and half centuries before the emergence of physiocracy in the mid-eighteenth century. But there is no agreement about its beginning. To some writers it started in the early sixteenth century, others date it still earlier (Whittaker, 1960, p. 31). The importance of mercantilism in the history of economic thought needs no explanation for students of the subject. It regarded bullion as money and trade as a source to obtain it. Historians of economic thought have explored the factors that helped the development of mercantilism. For example, Eric Roll (1974, pp. 54–5) mentions the following as some of the factors operating behind development of mercantilism:

> The growth of nation states, anxious to destroy both the particularism of feudal society and universalism of the spiritual power of Church which resulted in a greater concern for wealth and quickening of economic activities, the revolution in the methods of farming, maritime discoveries.

Similarly Oser and Blanchfield (1975, p. 8) attribute development of mercantilism to 'the self-sufficiency of the feudal community, growth of cities, flourishment of trade, discovery of gold in the Western Hemisphere, great geographical discoveries, rise of national states, etc'.

But reasons behind the rise of mercantilists *per se* have not been adequately investigated. For example, what caused the change in their thinking and why they felt the need to strengthen the national state? Of course, it would require a thorough study of the background and circumstances in which 'mercantilism' developed. The present writer is inclined to think that the motive for the rise of mercantilism lies in the stimulus that the scholastic writers, and through them the mercantilist writers, received from works of the Muslim scholars. For Muslims, trading has been a praiseworthy commercial activity since the very beginning. It might have been considered by European scholars a major source of their strength. Thus, they tried to monopolize it. They arrived at the conclusion that for defeating Muslims, they must pay attention to unity and strengthen the national government. Heckscher has rightly assigned to the second part of his work the title 'Mercantilism as a system of power'. According to Heckscher this power goal appeared under two guises: power *per se*, especially in a military sense, as well as the power to be achieved via national economic prosperity (Heckscher, 1954, Vol. 2, Ch. 2).

A study not directly related to mercantilism would seem to support the present writer's contention 'that mercantilism was an action and reaction against the Muslims'. In view of its importance and to provide the basis for further research in this direction, some extracts will be in order here:

In the rise of mercantilism, discovery of the new world is considered a significant factor that was done in search of gold or means for gold. 'In Columbus' mind gold was important as a means of furthering his sovereign's crusade to capture Jerusalem'[17] (Hamdani, 1994, p. 281). Discovery of new lands had no meaning for Columbus except as a stepping stone toward the Christians of East and Emperor of Cathay (ibid., p. 285).

'Gold, said Columbus, 'is a wonderful thing! Whoever possesses it is master of everything he desires. With gold, one can even get souls into paradise' (Roll, 1974, p. 65, in a letter from Jamaica dated 1503, quoted by Marx in *Zur Kratic der politischem Oconomie*, 1930, p. 162). This is just opposite to what some of the historians of economic thought want to make us believe. For example, to Eric Roll (1974, p. 63), 'The mercantilists demanded a state strong enough to protect the trading interest and to break down the many medieval barriers to commercial expansion'.

Examples of fund raising for this purpose are also not uncommon. 'Portugal's King Diniz sent an ambassador to Pope John XXII to solicit funds for the construction of fleet to be used against Muslims' (Hamdani, 1994, p. 286).

Disappointed from the conquest at the battlefield, mercantilists tried to block the Muslim power on the economic front: 'If one takes this trade of Malacca out of their [Mamluks'] hands, Cairo and Mecca will be entirely ruined, and to Venice no spices will be conveyed, except what her merchants go to buy in Portugal.' This was declared by Portuguese governor Alfonso de Albuquerque after conquering Goa and Malacca in 1511 (ibid., p. 288).[18] The establishment of a powerful Ottoman empire and its custody of the holy places of Islam made the Crusaders forget Jerusalem (ibid., p. 289). Perhaps Montgomery Watt also realizes this when he says, 'When the advancement to Jerusalem through the Mediterranean or eastern Europe was proved to be impracticable, a few men began to wonder if the Saracens (Muslims) could be attacked in the rear. . . . Certainly some of those who sponsored or participated in the exploring expeditions regarded these as Crusading enterprise, and the members of the expeditions bore the Crusaders' cross' (Watt, 1972, p. 57).

Thus, changing attitudes of Medieval Europe towards trade, as a result of an encounter with the Muslim scholars and rulers, the emergence of mercantilism was another turning point in the history of economic thought. O'Brien says: 'The extension of commercial life which took place about the beginning of the thirteenth century raised acute controversies about the legitimacy of commerce. Probably nothing did more to broaden the teaching on this subject than the necessity of justifying trade which became more and more insistent after the Crusades' (O'Brien, 1920, p. 147). However, one must remember an interesting difference. While the Muslims believed in trade as a source of mutual benefit, early mercantilist intellectuals believed like Aristotle that trade was a war because they held that one nation's gain would be at the cost of others. One man's gain is another man's loss. The French essayist Michel de Montaigne wrote in 1580: 'The profit of one man is the damage of another . . . No man profiteth but by the loss of others' (Oser and Blanchfield, 1975, p. 9). Jean Baptiste Colbert (d. 1683), 100 years after him felt that 'one nation can become rich only at the expense of another . . . Commerce is therefore a continual and a bitter war among nations for economic advantage' (ibid., p. 21). The mercantilists realized the mutual benefit from trading only after discovery of the theory of comparative cost advantage.

NOTES

1. See Baeck (1994, pp.112–14) for a detailed study of Ibn Rushd's ideas on money.
2. Salim Abu'l 'Ala. Secretary to Hisham b. Abd al-Malik (d.125/742). He translated

Aristotle's letters to Alexander – *Sirr al-Asrār*. It was translated to Latin by Philippus Tripolatanus in 1340 C.E. The Arabic text could be published in 1954 only after its English translation, which appeared 36 years ago.

3. *'Ikhwān al-Ṣafā* [Brothers of Purity] was a secret society in Basra, Iraq, founded around 340/951. They published 51 tracts known as the *Rasā'il 'Ikhwān al-Ṣafā*, which constituted an encyclopedia of knowledge in various sciences. Their Neoplatonic ideas, as well as the method whereby they would raise questions, but not answer them except indirectly and by implication and their particular belief, led them to be identified as Isma'ilis.
4. The final version of that *Sirr al-Asrār* was translated into Latin by Philippus Tripolatanus in 1340 C.E.
5. Abu al-Rabi' Najm al-Din Sulayman b. Abd al-Qawi al-Tufi (657–711/1259–1316). Born in the village of Tuf in the Iraqi state of Sarsar. In 691/1291 he came to Baghdad and migrated to Damascus in 704/1303. He died in the city of Khalil in Palestine. *Bughyat al-Sā'il fī Ummahāt al-Masā'il* and *Mi'rāj al-Wuṣūl* are two important books out of his many works still in manuscript.
6. Scholastics were an outgrowth of and having a different approach from Christian monastic teaching circles. European scholasticism was the outcome of a new type of school where Roman law and Greek philosophy was also studied. It prevailed during 1100–1500. To Viner (1978, p. 46), the term scholastic broadly covers 'all Catholic moral theologians and canonists who wrote in the central tradition of the Church from the late Middle Ages to the end of the sixteenth century.'
7. For an account of the scholastic deviation from early fathers on matters of economic interest, refer to Viner, 1978, pp. 106–11.
8. Greek philosophy was known to Christian scholars in their early period also. It never died fully among them. Even some translations were made directly from Greek to Latin. The reader may refer to Gordon (1975, pp. 82–110) to see how Christian fathers reacted to Greek ideas in early centuries. It was totally different from what they did after discovering it with Muslim commentaries.
9. In a recently published well-documented book, after proving that 'Aristotle (384–322 B.C.) was available to the West for 15 centuries (three centuries B.C. plus 12 centuries C.E.), in Greek, in Latin and even in some other tongues, and yet the West was sunk in barbarism' al-Djazairi (2005, p. 97) raises certain questions: 'Had he (Aristotle) been the source of all scientific knowledge, why did no awakening take place in Greece and Byzantium his land of birth and availability respectively? And why did neither today's Greece nor old Byzantium make the maritime discoveries . . . if Aristotle was the key? Why . . . did not the West understand the earth was round by just reading Aristotle in any century (15 of them) before he was translated from Arabic? Why did the West wait until Aristotle discovered in formerly Islamic lands (Toledo and Sicily) and in translations from Arabic in the twelfth century to understand this? And why did Western Christendom have to discover Aristotle in Arabic to understand all about philosophy, optics, physics, etc.?'
10. Schumpeter (1997) has mentioned the role of the Muslim scholars in his encyclopedic work *History of Economic Analysis* at the margin only. See pp. 87–8, footnote.
11. The Qur'an says: '. . . O you who believe! Observe your duty to Allah and give up what remains (due to you) from the *ribā*, if you are (in truth) believers. And if you do not, then be warned of war (against you) from Allah and His messenger. And if you repent, then you have your principal (without interest). Wrong not and you shall not be wronged' (2: 277).
12. During the recent financial crisis, many savants saw risk-sharing as a solution of the problem. In their opinion, the crisis originated due to financial institutions' effort to shift the risk to others (Chapra, 2009, p. 30).
13. Abu Is'haq Ibrahim b. Ali al-Shirazi (393–476/1002–1083). Lived in Baghdad and was a leading scholar of his time. When Nizam al-Mulk al-Tusi established the famous

university of Nizamiyah at Baghdad, he appointed him as head of this institution which he served until his death. *Al-Muhadhdhab* is his important work in jurisprudence.

14. '*Al- 'afw*' is also translated as what is beyond one's needs (see the translation of the verse in Ali, 1975, p. 86), or whatever one can spare (see the translation of the verse in Asad, 1980, p. 48).
15. Ghazanfar has tried to trace parallels and linkages between St Thomas Aquinas and Abu Hamid al-Ghazali, and has shown how the former's *Summa* and the latter's *'Iḥyā'* have parallel commentaries on compatible economic topics (Ghazanfar, 2003, pp. 193–203).
16. Watt (1972, pp. 85–92) who gives an incomplete list of Arabic words in English in eight pages writes, 'The . . . list contains English words which have passed through Arabic at some stage in their history. Many have come into Arabic from other languages. Since the chief interest of the list is to indicate our debt to medieval Islam, recent importations by travelers in Arab countries have been excluded.'
17. The statement is based on a direct quotation from Columbus' writing in which he addresses the Catholic Sovereign: 'I declared to your Highnesses that all the gain of this my Enterprise should be spent in the conquest of Jerusalem' (Morison, 1963, p. 139).
18. The fact that the major European countries jointly attacked Jerusalem and were defeated, may be the reason that mercantilism simultaneously developed in all these countries. Here we presented the case of Portuguese mercantilists only. There is a need to investigate about others on the same line. It seems that the movement that started on economic and religious grounds, turned into a completely economic movement and they fought against each other also later when their economic interests clashed.

8. Links between Muslim economic thought and the mainstream economics

8.1 CHANNELS OF CONTACT

Muslim scholars' influence on Medieval Europe with respect to philosophy, science, mathematics, geography, history, art and culture is well-documented and known in the circle of concerned subjects.[1] But their impact on economic thinking and institutions – a very important part of life – is yet to be fully explored and recognized. The very fact that Medieval Europe borrowed from Muslim scholars in so many diverse fields is enough to believe that they must not have missed the economic thought of the Muslim scholars as there was no reason to ignore their intellectual contribution in this vital field. In the preceding pages we documented the evidence of Muslim influence upon the medieval scholars. They used the available knowledge from the Muslim sources to advance their ideas and build their institutions.[2] The Muslim influence reached Medieval Europe through translations, education, oral transmission, accounts of travel, trade, crusades, diplomatic missions and pilgrimages. The following is a brief description of these channels.

8.1.1 Translation

Translations of Muslim scholars' contributions into European languages were the most important channel through which their ideas reached the West. It was a continuous process spanning over several centuries (starting from the eleventh century C.E. up to the fifteenth century). We have elaborated translation activities above in Chapter 2. But a few important points will also be in order here. Louis Baeck (1994, p. 119) identifies five important centers of translation of religious, philosophical and scientific texts. The first organized translation center was Tarazona, in Aragon.

1. In Castile, the translation center of Toledo was created by Archbishop Raimundo.

2. The Court of Emperor Fredrick II in Sicily played a prominent role.
3. Barcelona, the center of high culture in Catalonia's maritime economy.
4. Cultural centers like Perpignan, Narbonne, Nimes and Toulouse, were transmission belts of texts translated into old French.

The importance of Arabic translations into European languages and their role in the development of scholastic thought has been recognized by several economists (Schumpeter, 1997, pp. 87, 88; Gordon, 1975, p. 154) but the impression has been given that their role was just the transmitter of Greek ideas.[3] The fact is that with every translation they had also contributed their commentary, exposition, criticism and additions and the West benefited from all of these. Karl Pribram is perhaps among the few Western economists who have acknowledged it. He says: 'All relevant writings of the Greek philosopher Aristotle (384–322 B.C.) were gradually made available in Latin translation along with various treatises in which Arabian philosophers had interpreted Aristotle's work in light of their own reasoning. Of particular importance for subsequent development of Western thought was a translation into Latin of the commentaries of Aristotle's *Ethics* by the Cordoban philosopher Ibn-Rushd, called Averroes (1126–1198)' (Pribram, 1983, p. 4). He mentions two streams that affected Medieval society. The second and 'far more important stream started within the body of Scholastic theologians who derived their intellectual armory from the works of Arabian philosophers' (ibid., p. 2). In the assessment of Meyerhof, translations from Arabic which descended on barren scientific soil of Europe had the effect of fertilizing rain (Meyerhof, 1931, p. 351).

Translations of Arabic philosophers were used in Europe for many centuries as part of reading materials. The influence of the Muslim scholars evident from the fact that two schools of thought pertaining to Ibn Rushd, Parisian Averroists and Italian Averroists, were established (Langholm, 1998, p. 29).

8.1.2 Oral Transmission

Another important channel of transmission of Muslim thought had been through the European students who attended learning centers in Spain, Morocco, Egypt and other parts of the Muslim world. On their return they engaged in teaching, preaching or developing those disciplines. The oral transmission obviously could not be recorded. However, we find in history many important names, like Constantine, the African[4] and Adelard[5] of Bath (England) who traveled to Muslim countries, learned Arabic, studied there and brought back the newly acquired knowledge to Europe. Even

Pope Silvester II was educated among the Arabs of Toledo (Lopez-Baralt, 1994, p. 512).

Leonardo of Pisa whose work *Liber Abaci* is said to mark the beginning of economic analysis in Europe (Bernardelli, 1961), traveled and studied in Bougie in Algeria, and on his return he wrote the said book in 1202 (Watt, 1972, p. 63). The first Western universities were established on the pattern of Muslim seminaries.[6] The style of architecture of these universities, their curricula and their methods of instruction were similar to the Muslim seminaries (Sharif, 1966, p. 1368). Sometimes, they invited the Muslim scholars for promoting education. In the thirteenth century, the German emperor Frederic (1194–1250 C.E.) surrounded his court with Arabian philosophers (Pribram, 1983, p. 633n).

8.1.3 Trade and Commerce

Change in Medieval Christianity's outlook through trade, as noted earlier, was a manifestation of the influence of Muslim scholars. Enough evidence exists to show that trade was conducted from the Arab world through Russia to Poland, the shores of the Baltic seas to Scandinavia, to north central Europe. 'Series of hoards, containing many thousands of Muslim silver *dirhams* that have been found in the countries around the Baltic' (Lewis, 1970, p. 85) are proof of a vast trading network with the Muslim countries. With reference to a Russian jurist, Baron de Taube, Hamidullah states: 'when Arab traders came as far as Sweden and Denmark in the West and China in the East, there was "passivity on the part of Byzantine Greeks in domain of international commerce"; and as proof he argues to the fact that until 1914, "against 38000 pieces of Arab money found in Sweden , one counted only 200 pieces of Byzantine money in the same country"' (Hamidullah, 1968, para. 125, p. 68). According to Bernard Lewis: 'Italian and Spanish archives contain many documents relating commerce, including a number in Arabic' (ibid., 1970, p. 81). Many European cities and towns, especially in southern France and Italy, originated in the 'footsteps of trade' with the Mediterranean Arab-Islamic world (Krueger, 1961, p. 69). Genial papers of Egyptian Jewish provenance reflect commercial and social relations, which were by no means limited to Egypt but extended to the Mediterranean lands, eastwards to India (Lewis, 1970, p. 84). According to Goitein, during the high Middle Ages, the Mediterranean resembled a free trade community, goods, money and books traveling far and almost without restrictions throughout the area (Goitein, 1967, Vol. 1, p. 66).[7]

Trade being a praiseworthy occupation among the Muslims, with the advent of Islam the trading relation with the West was enhanced, not curtailed, in spite of so many ups and downs. Al-Tunisi (1967, p.105) quotes Duruy:[8] 'The Arabs were always keen on commerce, and when their influence extended from the Pyrenees (the mountains between France and Spain) to the Himalayas (in the northernmost part of India) they became the greatest merchants in the world'. Heaton observes: 'Muhammadanism regarded trade as a worthy occupation, ties of rule and religion facilitated long-distance trade and travel and since the Asiatic and the Moslem world possessed many industrial or agricultural skills and products which were superior to those of the European end, the West benefited by the lessons it learned from its new masters' (Heaton, 1948, p. 76). In fact, 'economic motive' led to an increased knowledge of the Muslim world to a large number of European merchants (Rodinson, 1974, p. 20). Commenting on the trade relation of the West with the Muslim East and its impact on cultural exchange, Haskins notes that it was never confined to the wares of commerce. 'We must remember that ever since the Greek and Phoenician traders it has been impossible to separate the interchange of wares from the interchange of knowledge and ideas' (Haskins, 1927, p. 64).

8.1.4 Crusades[9]

Many writers have emphasized the role of the Crusades in facilitating the contact between West and East and thus providing opportunities for the West to benefit from ideas and institutions of the Muslim East. According to Durant, a major reason behind the Crusades was the great desire of the Italian cities of Pisa, Genoa, Venice, Amalfi themselves (Durant, 1950, p. 586). Langholm admits that: 'The Crusades had opened up the world; towns and markets were expanding with the growing economies, new commercial techniques were being introduced' (Langholm, 1987, p. 115). However, like most of the contemporary writers he could not see the influence of the Muslim scholars in guiding norms of behavior in that important area. He ignored the effect of the Muslim philosophy and science – the real factor in the rise of scholasticism and considered it a 'synthesis of Roman law and Greek philosophy' (ibid., p. 115).

In the opinion of Heaton 'the Crusades came as a heaven-sent opportunity to establish firmer footholds in the meeting place of East and West" (Heaton, 1948, p. 152). As periods of peace were longer than periods of war, the Christians and the Muslims intermingled freely at social, economic and academic levels. The Crusades provided an important channel of communication between the West and the East. The Crusaders benefited not only from commercial products of the East but its economic institutions, and scientific ideas of Muslim scholars as well, such as *ḥisbah* [agoranomos], *muḍārabah* [commenda], *suftaja*, *ṣakk* [cheque], *tarīf* [tariff], etc. Realizing effectiveness of this channel, Pribram observes: 'The consolidation of economic views which took place in the thirteenth century was partly due to the fact that Crusaders had brought to the cities of Italy and some other European countries the knowledge of new methods of organizing industries and commercial activities' (Pribram, 1983, pp. 3–4). According to Krueger (1961, p. 72), the Crusades had 'the strongest influence on the development of medieval trade and industry.' Crusader coinage with Arabic inscriptions has been discovered which is an evidence of the Arab-Islamic influence.[10]

From the early Islamic period the Jews and the Christians lived peacefully in the Muslim lands and engaged in secretarial and translation work. Being followers of the same religion as the Western world, they enjoyed sympathy and respect and proved a link between the East and the West. They also worked as channel for transfer of the Muslim intellectual heritage to the West. Maimonides (Musa bin Maymun),[11] the Jewish scholar is an example of such links.

8.1.5 Travelers and Explorers

The curiosity to know the world other than in which man lives has been in all ages a driving force that induced people to go on exploration of other countries. One part of the Muslim world we have examples of are Nasir Khusraw,[12] Ibn Jubayr,[13] and Ibn Battutah. In addition to students and traders who traveled to the Muslim lands in search of knowledge and useful commodities, a number of adventurers toured the East, saw people and the economy, studied their ideas and institutions and on return recorded such events for the benefit of their countrymen. We have memoirs of Jean de Joinville (d. 1317) advisor of King Louis IX, who accompanied him in the Crusade of 1248. We also have the travel account of Venetian explorer Marco Polo (d. 1324). Durant (1950, p. 979) notes that Raymond Lull (d. 1315) the Dominican monk toured extensively in the Arab world and wrote several works in the Arabic language. His aim was to engage in 'missionary work among Saracens and Jews'. The Englishman Adelard of Bath (d. 1152) is another notable traveler who is identified by Haskins (1927, p. 20) as 'the pioneer student of Arabic science and philosophy in the twelfth century.' These and other travel accounts became a channel for transmission of knowledge about ideas and institutions that existed in the East, and they must have impressed the curious readers creating an urge to adopt them.

8.1.6 Diplomatic Channel

Diplomatic relations also provided an opportunity to learn from the advanced nations of the East. 'Charlemagne was in diplomatic relations with the caliph of Baghdad, Harun al-Rashid, as well as with the latter's enemy, the Umayyad emir of Spain; and by this channel some knowledge of the vastness and power of the Islamic world might have reached Europe' (Watt, 1972, p. 13). Most of the European kings had good relations with the Mamluk sultans of Egypt. Pope John XXII sent a letter to Sultan Nasir bin Qalawun in 1327, asking him to treat the Christians of the East with benevolence and care. Nasir agreed to his request (Muir, 1896, p. 5). A similar letter to Sultan Nasir was sent in the same year by Charles IV (1322–1328), the King of France, about the welfare of the Christians residing in his sultanate (Lane-Poole, 1925, p. 310).

8.1.6 Pilgrimage

Pilgrimage of European Christians and Jews to holy places in Palestine and Syria and other shrines in the Muslim lands provided opportunity to all sections of the society to interact and learn from the local Muslims. Watt (1972, p. 14) mentions a few such shrines in Palestine and Spain where a regular pilgrim route had been established. Sarton states: 'Pilgrims were especially numerous because it was now a well established custom in Christendom to start on a pilgrimage to obtain indulgences or the remission of sins. So many were the pilgrims that hospices were built to accommodate them, as on the Alpine and Pyrenean passes (some of these hospices were much older). The influence of these pilgrims cannot be overestimated. The pilgrimage roads stand in the same relation to the intellectual and artistic development of Christendom as the commercial roads to its economic organization' (Sarton, 1927–1948, Vol. 2, p. 131). According to Gabrieli, envoys, travelers, and pilgrims were the first to bring news to Europe of the existence of Muslim culture and science; and most of all, the collective contact between the Muslim and the Christian communities in the areas of mixed population on the borders between the two worlds, that revealed to Christendom the wealth of cultural attainments of which the Arabs were now the depositories, the promoters and transmitters (Gabrieli, 1970, p. 851).

8.1.7 Monasteries and Cathedral Schools

Monastery libraries housed voluminous translated works of the Arab-Islamic scholars. According to Artz (1953, p. 229), 'alongside the monastery as a center of culture was the cathedral school . . . to them was brought most of the science and philosophy from the Byzantines and Saracens.' In accumulation of and dissemination of Islamic sciences, the influence of cathedral schools was especially very important in Lorraine and Spain (Haskins, 1927; Cochrane, 1994). In the opinion of Hill (1993, p. 220), it was from the cathedral schools that the universities were to be established, and it was from the cathedral schools and early universities that the Islamic knowledge was to enter the Latin West. Christian Spain welcomed the cultural influences which came from the south (Muslim Spain) through Mozarabs (Christians under Muslim rule), intermediaries who migrated from the Islamic territories. They contributed to the restoration of monasteries. Due to their knowledge of Arabic and local Latin dialects the Mozarabs played an important role in transfer of Arab-Islamic sciences to the Christian world through translation and oral transmission (Metlitzki, 1977, p. 6).

8.1.8 Royal Courts

The royal courts were 'as brilliant and refined a center of Arab learning as any in the Middle East or in Spain' (Menocal, 1985, p. 75). Some of the Christian rulers entrusted education and training of their sons to Muslim tutors (Briffault, 1928, pp. 198 and 202). In spite of Christian kings' fierce fighting against the Islamic foe on the battle fields, many European royal courts and monarchies patronized the Islamic heritage of science and culture. In this respect, Lindberg (1978, p. 78) mentions names of the Carolingian court of Charles the Bald (d. 877), Frederick II (d. 1250) and Manfred in Sicily (d. 1266), the Angevin court in Naples, and the courts of Alfonso X (d. 1284), in Castile and James II in Aragon (d. 1327).[14]

8.1.9 Missionaries

Efforts by missionaries also played a role in the transfer of Islamic learning to the West. As an example, in about 1246, Raymond Lull (d. 1315) entered the personal service of James the Conqueror, the king of Aragon, before becoming tutor to the king's two sons – Peter and James. For nine years, from 1265 to 1274, he lived in Majorca, Spain, studying Arabic with a Muslim slave. Later on he traveled considerably in Western Europe, to Montpellier, France, in particular, and Rome, lecturing in universities, attending religious conferences, trying to interest popes and kings in his projects (Sarton, 1924, Vol. 2, p. 900). According to Sauvaget (1965, p. 228), 'Islamic culture was known in Europe partly through the commercial markets, sometimes through the travels of Christian missionaries in the East.'

To conclude, we can say that there were numerous channels of communication available between the East and the West and there were far greater reasons for Medieval Europe to be influenced by economic ideas of the Muslim scholars. The movement of search for and diffusion of knowledge in the medieval times was complete opposite to what we have today. At that time, the place of the Muslim world for the West was what at present the place of the West is for the Muslim world.

8.2 CONTRIBUTIONS OF THE MUSLIM SCHOLARS FORM PART OF THE FAMILY TREE OF ECONOMICS

Some textbooks give a family tree of economics and its development in diagrammatic form. It will be interesting to study such family trees and trace the location of the Muslim economic thought.[15] For the sake of convenience we choose to discuss only two works, *Economics* by Paul Samuelson (1976), and *A History of Economic Thought* by John Fred Bell (1967). It may be noted that Adam Smith is a common ancestor in all the family trees.

Samuelson's *Economics*, was first published in 1948. Up to the 11th edition (1980) it had a family tree that showed Aristotle and the Bible as the originating point from where the scholastics emerged; St Thomas acquired representative personality and created mercantilists and physiocrats. The mercantilists also had roots in earlier practitioners. Both physiocracy and mercantilism ended with Adam Smith (see 'Family Tree of Economics' in Samuelson, 1976, inside back title).

From its 12th edition, William D. Nordhaus joined as co-author of the book. The family tree of economics was also changed to begin from physiocrats and mercantilists (Samuelson and Nordhaus, 1985). In the 17th edition (2001) they removed the tree altogether.

Bell shows contributory currents in evolution of the economic thought. From Biblical times up to Adam Smith, main-stream economic thought passed through the Middle Ages comprising the church, Aquinas, and scholasticism which had a direct relationship with the Greek philosophers and the Roman law-givers. The other points of mainstream are the 'rise of national states', the'beginning of modern capitalism' (to which are related French Colbertism and German Cameralism), English mercantilism and physiocrats (Bell, 1967, p. 9). Except for physiocrats, others were various elements of mercantilism as is testified by textbooks of economic thought. In essence, both authors depict the same idea except that Bell's figure is more elaborate. Of course, one cannot expect Professor Samuelson to mention the contribution of the Muslim scholars in the family tree of economics despite his rightful claim to the 'latest thinking of modern economists' (Samuelson and Nordhaus, 2001, p. xvii) and 'innovations in economics itself' (ibid., p. xviii). He could not take notice of the modern development of Islamic economics and 'innovation in banking and finance' on a participatory basis. But one must have expected Bell to include contribution of the Muslim scholars in contributory currents in the development of economic thought (Bell, 1967, p. 9) as he himself has noted that the scholastics accepted 'the newly discovered Greek and Moslem philosophy and science' (ibid. p. 43). This is amazing because he does not concentrate on the mainstream economics only and also mentions the related currents. Does the contribution of the Muslim scholars not deserve a place even in related currents?

From the foregoing it is obvious that any family tree of economics would be incomplete without assigning a part to the Muslim scholars who translated, discussed, improved and transferred Greek ideas to scholastic scholars. In the preceding pages, we have seen considerable original contribution of the Muslim scholars to economic thought and the manner they transferred the whole treasure of knowledge to Europe through a number of channels. They were a connecting link between the Greek originators and the scholastic followers.

Greek ideas, with the medium of the Muslim scholars, helped not only in the rise of scholastics, but also contributed their influence in later centuries. Raymond de Roover (1976, pp. 333–4) has presented documentary evidence that Adam Smith used scholastic ideas in formulating his economic thought. Lowry quotes the example of 'Xenophon's *Ways and Means,* a mid-fourth century B.C. proposal for developing the Athenian economy, which was added as an appendix to the 1698 edition of Davenant's treatise on trade and to the 1751 edition of Petty's *Political Arithmetic*' (Lowry, 1987, pp. 8–9). 'There has never been a period when the works of Plato and Aristotle have not been studied in European universities' (ibid., p. 9). So what can we say about the commentaries of Averroes on *Nicomachean Ethics* and *Politics*? This influence continued until the emergence of Smith's economics. Lowry quotes a contemporary of Adam Smith saying that 'both the *Theory of Moral Sentiments* and the *Wealth of Nations*' issued from the womb of the classics'.[16] Another of his contemporaries argued that Greek sources 'constituted an essential and fundamental element in establishing of several of [Smith's] central positions', and they 'in fact constitute, not alone the starting point in documentation, but the foundation of the whole' (ibid., p. 10).[17]

Contributions of the Muslim scholars came after the Greeks in the family tree of economics. They were the main cause not only of the birth of scholastic economic ideas but also the rise of mercantilism, as shown in the previous chapter. The scholastic ideas do not match well in terms of coverage, quality and originality to the Islamic tradition in economic thought. As regards St Thomas Aquinas who is considered the most outstanding scholastic scholar, Copleston, a historian of medieval philosophy observes 'The fact that Aquinas derived ideas and stimulus from a variety of sources tend to suggest both that he was an eclectic and that he was lacking in originality. For when we consider this or that doctrine or theory, it is very often possible to make claims such as, "this comes straight from Aristotle", "that has already been said by Avicenna" or "that is obviously a development of an argument used by Maimonides". In other words, the more we know about Aristotle and about Islamic and Jewish philosophy, as also of course about previous Christian thought, the more we may be inclined to wonder what, if anything is peculiar to Aquinas himself' (Copleston, 1972, p. 181, quoted by Mirakhor, 1987, p. 248–9).

8.2.1 A Family Tree of Islamic Economics

Before we suggest a proper structure of economics as such, we would like to draw a chart of Islamic economics (see Figure 8.1) to show convergence and divergence between the mainstream economics and the Islamic economics.

The above mentioned family tree of Islamic economic thought depicts its rise from the beginning up to its modern development. The present treatise provides an explanation up to the 1500 C.E. period, which after that largely remained unexplored. The modern development of Islamic economics came as a response to the challenge posed by materialistic systems – capitalism and Marxism. However, this is beyond the scope of this study.

8.2.2 Place of Muslim Scholars in the Family Tree of Mainstream Economics

The fact that scholastic scholars got Greek ideas through the medium of the Muslim scholars and based their ideas on Greek philosophy and its commentary presented by Muslim philosophers, and the fact that mercantilism came as a result of Muslim influence, the contribution of the Muslim scholars deserves a place in development of mainstream economics. And they must be rehabilitated for the sake of doctrinal continuity and objectivity, academic honesty and justice. A correct family tree of economics is given in Figure 8.2.

However, the idea of family tree may not be plausible to some readers because the word 'family' points toward harmony and resemblance

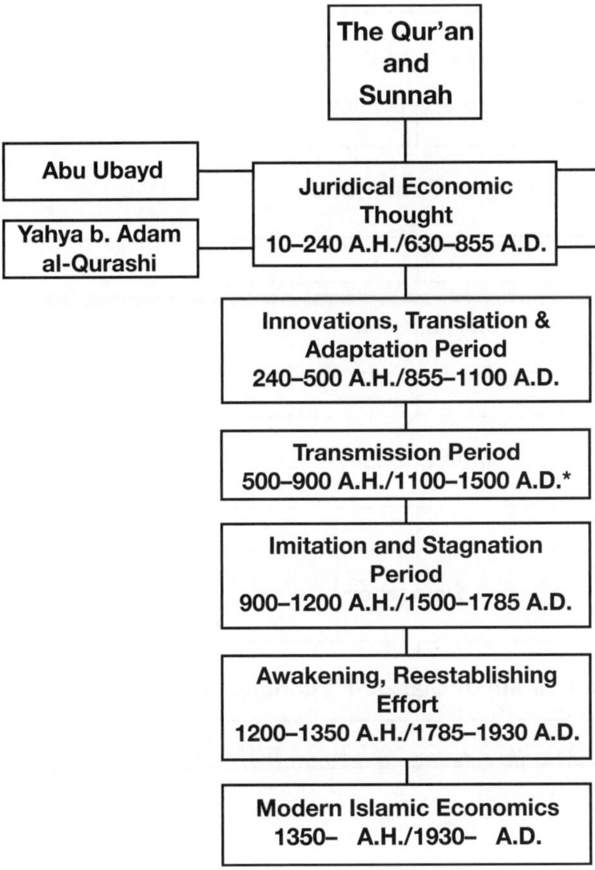

Note: Dates are rounded and roughly corresponding, not exactly
*In this work we have studied up to the ninth/fifteenth century only.

Figure 8.1 Development chart of Islamic economics

between successors and predecessors.[18] But the apprehension is not well-founded. We find least similarity between scholastics and mercantilism. Physiocracy has no relation with mercantilism. Adam Smith attacked both mercantilism and physiocracy.

A better presentation of a family tree should demonstrate development of economics with various influences that worked behind it. This is important in the case of Muslim economic thought. Other systems merged with the new ones or vanished altogether, but the Islamic economic thought maintained its identity. It was eclipsed for a long period but never died,

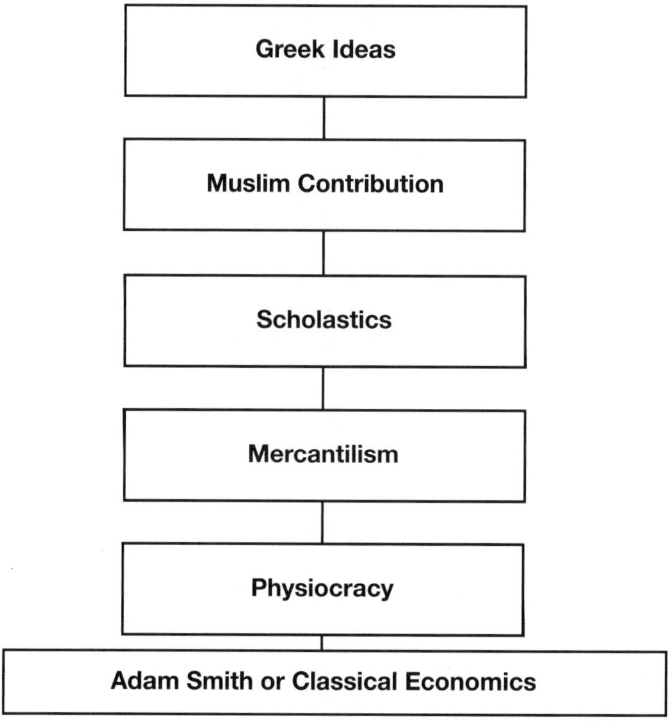

Figure 8.2 Place of Muslim scholars in the family tree of mainstream economics

and that is the reason it has re-emerged in the twentieth century with full vigor. Perhaps this is the right time for its re-emergence, as the conventional materialistic self-seeking economics could not satisfy aspirations of humanity. See the flow chart in Figure 8.3[19] which shows the interaction and influence of Islamic economics from the beginning up to the modern period.

8.3 BORROWING WITHOUT ACKNOWLEDGEMENT

Borrowing by the scholastic philosophers from the Muslim scholars in the economic field is the least recognized fact in spite of convincing circumstantial evidences.[20] The main reason could be that the scholastic scholars

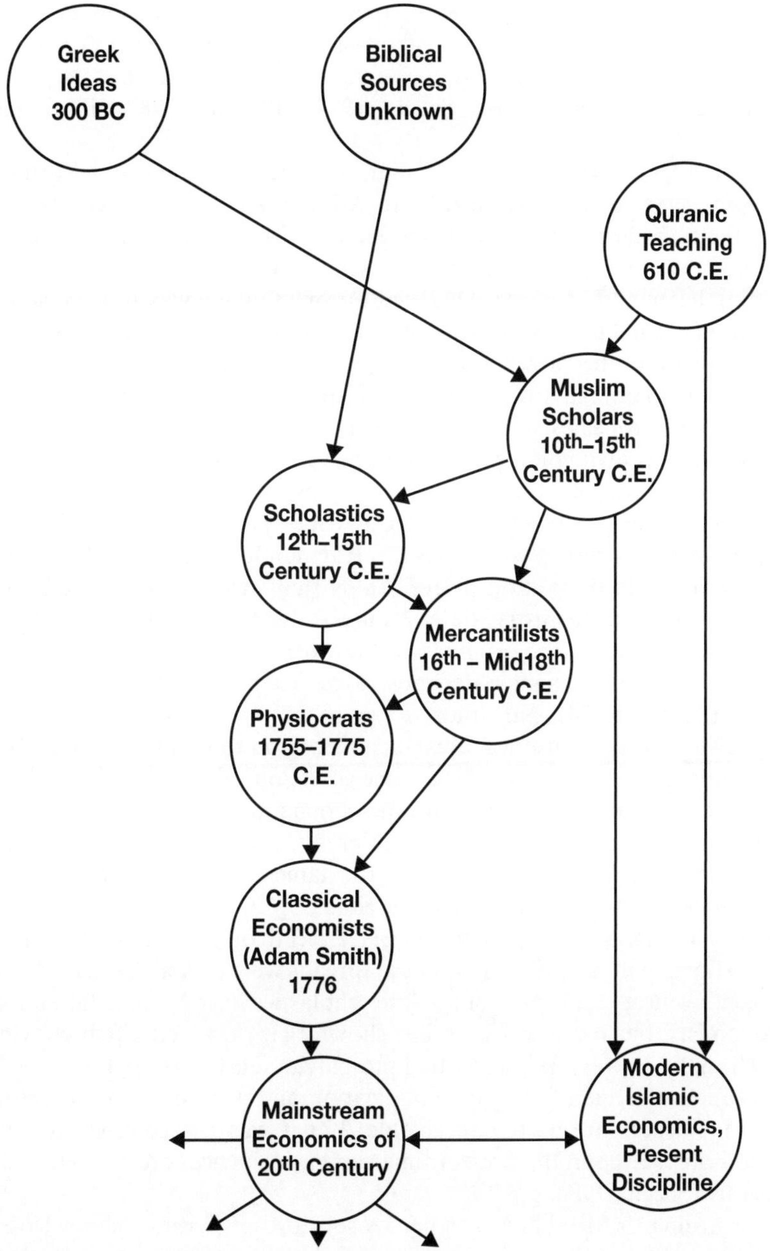

Figure 8.3 *Interaction and influence of Islamic economics from beginning up to the modern period*

never cited the Islamic sources in their discourse on economic issues. The question arises why did the scholastics not acknowledge borrowing from the Muslim scholars? A few contemporary writers have tried to answer this (see, for example, Sezgin, 1984; Mirakhor, 1987; Ghazanfar, 1995).

First, the scholastics held a denigrating view of Islam and Muslims (Sezgin, 1984, p. 127). According to Mirakhor (1987, p. 262), 'To say that the crusaders epitomized this negative attitude is an understatement'. Without naming names, he quotes a scholar who suggests that in denigrating Islam and Muslims, Medieval Europe found a way to form a new image of itself. 'Because Europe was reacting against Islam, it belittled the influence of the Saracens and exaggerated its dependence on its Greek and Roman heritage' (ibid., pp. 262–3). In the fourteenth century a large number of European scholars studied translations of the Arabic books and prepared their own volumes or summary, in which they not only dropped names of the Muslim authors but gave all credit to those Greek scholars who were occasionally referred in those works (Sezgin, 1984, p. 127).

Here is an example given by Sezgin. Raymundus Lullus (d. 1315) spent his whole life in opposition of everything that was Arabic. He authored several books on chemistry. Later on it was discovered that most of these were translations of the original Arabic works. Even many such writers gave the slogan: 'Emancipate knowledge from the clutches of Arabs' (Sezgin, 1984, p. 34). No doubt a few scholars tried to do justice and acknowledged the Muslim scholars' contribution to various sciences. But discrediting forces dominated the scene (ibid., pp. 34–5).

Removal of names of the Muslim scholars and discarding their citation was also motivated by taking self-credit. There are several examples where the medieval scholars removed the name of the Muslim author and presented the book in their own name (ibid., pp. 33, 96, 128–9). Langholm states that after the war, famine and Black Death of the fourteenth century that left a gap in the primary sources, 'threads were picked up again in the fifteenth century and some of the late scholastics have become famous as economists, but recent research has shown that they were often copying verbatim from previously forgotten pre-plague sources' (Langholm, 1987, p. 116). In the age of slow communication and absence of print media, such incidences are quite conceivable. But it was not confined to that period only. Even in the present time similar incidences are noticed occasionally (Sezgin, 1984, p. 123).[21]

According to Mirakhor, another reason for not finding acknowledgement is that 'borrowing without acknowledgement seems to have been an accepted and a general practice among the scholastics' (Mirakhor, 1987, p. 263).[22] He cites many examples of such borrowing without acknowledgement within the scholastics themselves. It was very common while borrowing from the Muslim scholars. Many chapters of al-Ghazali's *'Iḥyā' ʿUlūm al-Dīn* were copied by Bar Heraeus, a minister of the Syriac Jacobite Church in thirteenth century (ibid., p. 263). Margaret Smith, in her work *al-Ghazali: The Mystic*, has shown convincing evidence of St Thomas' borrowing from al-Ghazali's work *'Iḥyā' ʿUlūm al-Dīn*. She compares the works of the two scholars and finds that in many cases 'St. Thomas uses the very words of al-Ghazali.' There is similarity between themes and arguments of the two works (Smith, 1944, pp. 220–2).[23] It may be remembered that al-Ghazali's *'Iḥyā'* is the main source of his economic ideas.

Finally, citation and acknowledgement depended on the nature of material targeted at and used by the scholastic scholars. In the words of Mirakhor, 'if there were any ideas in the writings and teachings of the Muslim scholars which were either dogma positive or dogma neutral with respect to Christianity, the scholastics borrowed with openness'. 'In this case, these ideas were borrowed without the scholastics necessarily acknowledging the source' (Mirakhor, 1987, p. 264). As far as ideas that were contrary to Christianity – dogma negative – they were rejected in the strongest possible terms while the bearer of the idea was criticized by name (ibid.).

As a whole, various possible relationships between ideas of the Muslim scholars, Greek philosophy and Christianity – hence scholastics' stand towards borrowing without acknowledgement or rejection – may be explained with the help of the following diagram (Figure 8.4).

Numbers 1, 2, 3 show specific ideas of each identity which are opposed to each other. No. 4 shows ideas that are common between the Muslims and the Greeks but alien to Christianity. Number 5 shows teachings which are common to Muslims and Christianity, while No. 6 shows ideas common between Christianity and Greek philosophy but alien to the Islamic tradition. Number 7 shows ideas which are common to all the three systems.

In the case of categories 1, 2, 3 , the Muslim scholars tried to interpret the Greek ideas for a possible synthesis. Otherwise, they criticized and refuted them. Since Christianity also faced the same problems, the scholastic scholars borrowed those arguments if they found them favorable, but did not acknowledge them. These were mainly philosophical and metaphysical ideas. However, if the scholastics perceived interpretation of a Muslim scholar as a threat to the Christian dogma, they were quick to point out the error with reference to him.

The same was the case in categories 4 and 6. They formed part of 'dogma negative'. The Muslim scholars were condemned by name. For

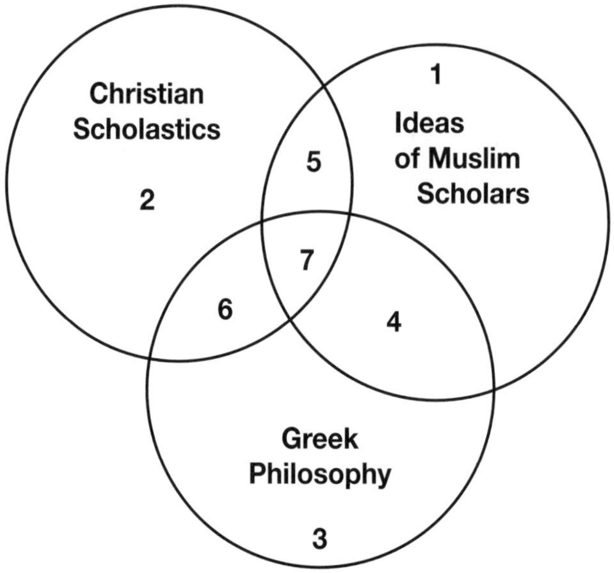

Figure 8.4 Kinds of relationship between ideas of the Muslim scholars, Christian scholastics and Greek philosophy

example, in 1277, Stephen Tampier, Bishop of Paris, published a list of Averroes's ideas which were condemned by him (Durant, 1950, pp. 957–8). Thomas Aquinas was led to write his *Summa* to halt the threatened liquidation of Christian theology by Arabic interpretations of Aristotle (ibid., p. 913). 'Indeed the industry of Aquinas was due not to love of Aristotle but to fear of Averroes' (ibid., p. 954). It was an acknowledgement but with ill-intention. Such references are not uncommon even in the contemporary texts, that fully ignore the Muslim scholars' contributions to economic thought. For example, while fully ignoring the Muslim contribution to economic thought, Roll refers to them as '. . . Moslems who had begun as raiding warriors . . .' (Roll, 1974, p. 42). Even Arabs' favorable attitude toward individual property right, is to Ashley 'self-seeking of pagans' (Ashley, 1893, p. 128) – a phrase perhaps borrowed from the scholastics, alluding to Muslims. Whittaker does not bother to register the Muslim scholars' contribution to economic thought but he does not forget to remind that, 'the spread of the Mohammedan power had not only threatened the existence of the eastern or Byzantine empire, centered on Constantinople, but having conquered northern Africa the Mohammedans had also spread into Spain and Sicily' (Whittaker, 1960,

p. 21). He says again: 'For a harassing and risky overland trade with Asia there was substituted a relatively easy sea route, which moreover, was free from menace by the Mohammedans' (ibid., p. 22).

Category 5 is kind of 'dogma positive' which was fully borrowed from the Muslim scholars without acknowledgement. For instance, 'the Spanish Dominican Monk, Raymond Martini,[24] borrowed many of al-Ghazali's ideas taken from *Tahāfut al-Falāsifah, al-Maqāṣid, al-Munqidh, Mishkāt al-'Anwār* and *'Iḥyā',* again without reference' (Sharif, 1966, p. 1361). Arnold and Guillaume (1931, p. 273) write: 'It was Raymund Martin who perceived the value of Algazel's *Tahāfut al-Falāsifah*, or Incoherence of the Philosophers, and incorporated a great deal of it which is polemic against the philosophers and scholastics in Islam, into his *Pugio Fedei.*'

Category 7 forms 'dogma neutral'. In this case also, as noted above, the scholastics borrowed without hesitation and referred to Greek scholars if they felt such a need. In the words of Daniel (1975, pp.176–7): 'There was a spontaneous and determined general agreement about what to take and what to reject; what was taken was always either culturally common or culturally neutral. The body of scientific knowledge was culturally neutral. Its cultural bearings were easily absorbed because they were part of the common inheritance of the Arab world and of Europe.' It may be noted that most of the economic ideas belonged to category 6 and 7 and were adopted by the scholastics without acknowledgement. However, denial of a debt or forgetting it does not cancel it.

NOTES

1. For example, Robert Briffault (1876–1948) writes:

> 'Science is the most momentous contribution of Arab civilization to the modern world . . . It was not science only which brought Europe back to life. Other and manifold influences from the civilization of Islam communicated its first glow to European life' (Briffault (1919), *Making of Humanity*, p. 202, cited in Iqbal, 2006, p. 130).

> 'For although there is not a single aspect of European growth in which the decisive influence of Islamic culture is not traceable, nowhere is it so clear and momentous as in the genesis of that power which constitutes the permanent distinctive force of the modern world, and the supreme source of its victory – natural science and the scientific spirit' (ibid., p. 190, cited in Iqbal, 2006, p. 130).

> 'The debt of our science to that of the Arabs does not consist in startling discoveries of revolutionary theories; science owes a great deal more to Arab culture, it owes its existence. . . . What we call science arose in Europe as a result of a new spirit of inquiry, of new methods of investigation, of the method of experiment, observation, measurement, of the development of Mathematics in a form unknown to the Greeks.

That spirit and those methods were introduced into the European world by the Arabs' (ibid.)

'It was under their successors at the Oxford School that Roger Bacon learned Arabic and Arabic Science. Neither Roger Bacon nor his later namesake has any title to be credited with having introduced the experimental method. Roger Bacon was no more than one of the apostles of Muslim science and method to Christian Europe; and he never wearied of declaring that knowledge of Arabic and Arabic Science was for his contemporaries the only way to true knowledge. Discussions as to who was the originator of the experimental method . . . are part of the colossal misrepresentation of the origins of European civilization. The experimental method of Arabs was by Bacon's time widespread and eagerly cultivated throughout Europe' (p. 202, cited in Iqbal, 2006, p. 130 (ibid).

According to Sharif, Muslim philosophy has influenced Medieval Europe in the following ways. It initiated humanistic movement, introduced the historical sciences and the scientific methods, helped the Western scholastics in harmonizing philosophy with faith, stimulated Western mysticism, laid foundation of the Italian Renaissance and to a degree molded the modern European thought down to the time of Immanuel Kant in certain directions even later (Sharif, 1966, Vol. 2, p. 1349).

2. 'In the transition from Late Antiquity to the Emergence of Latin West in the twelfth century, Islam was at its apogee and played an eminent role . . .' (Baeck, 1994, p. 95). Abbas Mirakhor (1987) refers to a number of works that establish beyond doubt Muslim scholars' influence on the great scholastics of the Medieval West (1987, p. 260 and p. 268 footnote). Again, C.R.S. Harris (1954, p. 40), an expert of the Medieval thought, writes: 'Without the influence of the Arabian peripateticism, the theology of Aquinas is unthinkable as his philosophy.'
3. A few authors have mentioned the Muslim scholars' role as 'translators, interpretators' and 'transmitters' of Greek ideas. But that is only to belittle their contribution and omit their place in the development of economic thought. They enriched economic thinking with new ideas and concepts. For verification, see the foregoing chapters on 'Islamic tradition in economic thought'.
4. Constantine the African. His original name is unknown, according to usual accounts, he earned a livelihood as a merchant traveling between Tunisia and southern Italy, perhaps dealing in drugs. On a visit to Salerno he realized how backward the school there was and for reasons unknown to us decided to go and study medicine in the Islamic world. He spent the final part of his life at the Benedictine monastery of Monte Casino, translating into Latin the medical works he had studied (Watt,1972, pp. 59–60).
5. Adelard of Bath, twelfth century English scholastic philosopher and translator from Arabic, was one of the most prominent writers on scientific subjects of his time in England. His translations include astronomical tables of al-Khwarizmi and *Elements* of Euclid, which for centuries served as the chief geometry textbook in the West. He traveled in Italy, Cilicia (an ancient region of Anatolia, which extends inland from the southeastern coast of modern Turkey, due north and northeast of the island of Cyprus), Syria, Palestine and Spain before returning to Bath in England and becoming a teacher of the future king Henry II.
6. In one of his articles George Makdisi (2000, p. 1) has shown the structural parallelism between the Islamic *waqf* and European forms of charitable foundations. It is note worthy that 'the charitable trust was the basis of all the early colleges in the Christian West, as in Islam, East and West. In London, the Church-Inns and the Inns of Court, and in Paris, the College des Dix-Huit, were all charitable trust foundations'.
7. Victor Duruy (1811–1894), the author of *Histoire du moyen age depuis la chute de l'empire d'occident jusqu'au milieu de Xve siecle* (Paris, 1867), from which the cited passage was translated by al-Tunisi (1967, pp. 122–8), authored a great number of

books on general history. He was minister of education in France from 1863 to 1869.

8. Based on various sources, Al-Djazairi (2005, pp. 413–15) establishes that: 'Islamic literature in the field of trade influenced subsequent Western literature, and by "coincidence", the Italian first. For instance, al-Dimashqi's *Kitāb* shows a very close relationship in technique and approach to the subsequent Pegalotti's *Practica della Mercatura* (N.Stilman in discussion seminar of published articles on Islam and the medieval West; in K.I. Semaan (ed.), 1980, p. 597). A great deal of the merchandise referred to in the two manuscripts are the same, and so is a lot of technical terminology, including the advice to businessmen, and so are many of the forms of business relationships (ibid).
9. The invading forces and Europe profoundly benefited from the Crusades. But for the Muslim East they had disastrous effects.
10. See also Bates, Michael L. (1989), 'Crusade Coinage with Arabic Inscriptions' in Kenneth Meyer Setton (1990) (ed.), *A History of the Crusades*, Madison, WI: University of Wisconsin Press, 6: 421–82.
11. Musa b. Maymun (525–607/1135–1204), known in Europe as Maimonides. Born in Cordova, Spain, who migrated with his family to Fez in 1160, around 1165 he traveled to Egypt and joined the court of Sultan as physician: He was appointed chief judge of the Jewish community in Egypt where he lived until the end of his life.
12. Nasir Khusraw (394–452/1003–1060). Born in a city near Balkh in Turkistan. Traveled a number of countries in seven years during 1045 to 1052. He gives a good account of economic condition of countries he visited which is helpful in understanding the economic ideas behind their economic policies and behavior.
13. Muhammad b. Ahmad Ibn Jubayr (540–614/1145–1214). Born in Valencia, a city of Andalus and died in Alexandra, traveled a number of countries on his way to Hijaz. His fame rests on his account of this fairly eventual journey, the *Riḥlah*. In his travel account he gives different economic provisions in countries he toured. The work is a very useful source for economic history and to derive economic ideas from it.
14. Al-Djazairi (2005, pp. 178–84) gives a detailed account of the role of these and some other European rulers in patronizing and dissemination of Islamic culture and science in their territories.
15. Ingrid Rima (1991) provides a detailed flow chart of pre-classical economics in her work *Development of Economic Analysis* but the link to Muslim scholars is missing. Paul Wonnacott and Ronald Wonnacott (1986) in their work *Economics* give a flow chart entitled 'Our Intellectual Heritage' on the inside title, and Oser and Blanchfield (1975) in their work *The Evolution of Economic Thought*, 3rd edn, pp. 94–5. Both works start from the Mercantilists.
16. Professor Lowry quotes Charles Fay (1956), *Adam Smith and Scotland of His Day*, Cambridge, Cambridge University Press.
17. He quotes William R. Scott (1949), pp. 79–99.
18. Those who like to make such a family tree can contend that the lineage tree does not necessitate similar belief or harmony in thinking. There is the example of Prophet Noah and his non-believing son.
19. Looking at Figure 8.3 one may ask whether twentieth century Islamic economists are directly influenced by the fifteenth century Muslim scholars? What about the interim period? In fact, the subsequent centuries saw a chain of scholars who discussed economic problems of their age. For example: al-Suyuti, Ibn Nujaym, Khunji, etc. in the sixteenth century, Katib Chalapi, al-Ramli, Sirhindi, etc. in the seventeenth century, Ibn Abd al-Wahhab, Shah Wali-Allah al-Dihlawi, and Uthman dan Fodio in the eighteenth century. However, born in a declining phase of the Muslim culture and sciences, only a few of them were creative thinkers. In the nineteenth century a kind of re-thinking and revival started. No doubt, this was result of a direct contact with the West. Hence, influence of the West has played an important role in this revival. For details refer to the following works of the author:

    a. *Muslim Economic Thinking and Institutions in the 10th A.H./16th C.E. Century*;

b. *A Study of Muslim Economic Thinking in the 11th A.H./17th C.E. Century*;
c. *Islamic Economic Thinking in the 12th A.H./18th C.E. Century: With Special Reference to Shah Wali-Allah al-Dihlawi*;
d. *Muslim Economic Thinking in the 19th Century – Part One Arab World.*

20. For example, scholastics based their economics on Greek ideas which were available with Arab commentaries and their additions. Langholm realizes that the Aristotelian tradition is no more Aristotle than is neo-classical classical or post-Keynesianism is Keynes. He is aware that 'the Aristotelianism of the Medieval period was to a great extent influenced by Muslim scholars as he traces the origin of value theory to Averroes' (Mirakhor, 1987, p. 262). Scholastics' immediate predecessors had nothing of economic sort. Documentary evidence is available on their influence in other sciences. There existed a very close parallel between economic ideas of scholastics and those of the Muslim scholars. Almost all scholastic scholars, mentioned by Schumpeter, were aware of and influenced by the Muslim philosophers.
21. Unfortunately, the evil of plagiarism has also been detected among a few contemporary writers of of Islamic economics. In the opinion of a leading scholar 'plagiarism is an endemic disease afflicting scholarship' (Siddiqi, 2008, p. 7). To him there are indicators that 'it is assuming bothersome proportions'.
22. It was also found among the Muslim scholars. For example, both Abu Yala al-Farra and al-Mawardi had a work entitled *al-Aḥkām al-Sulṭānīyah*, and the contents are almost the same. They were contemporaries. It is not known who wrote first and who borrowed. Another example: Ibn al-Qayyim (1953) incorporated the whole treatise of his teacher Ibn Taymiyah (1976) on *al-ḥisbah* in his book *al-Ṭuruq al-Ḥukmīyah*. No doubt, on certain occasions he referred to his *shaykh*, Ibn Taymiyah.
23. Guillaume (1931, pp. 279, 280) remarks: 'The resemblances between Averroes and St Thomas are so numerous that must be traceable to something firmer than mere coincidence.' He presents examples in his support. In many cases, it was not only the thinking of scholastics that was similar to that of the newly discovered savants, the Muslim scholars and jurists; the contents and style of their works also had a very close resemblance with those of the Muslim scholars. For example St Thomas Aquinas (d. 1274) devotes two chapters in his famous work *Summa Theologica* on elimination of cheating and usurious practices from buying and selling (Aquinas, 1947, II: II Q77 and Q78). Al-Ghazali devotes Chapter 3 of volume 2 of his work *'Iḥyā' ʿUlūm al-Dīn* to deal with business ethics [*adāb al-maʿāsh*] (al-Ghazali, n.d., Vol. 2, pp. 62–80). The two works have tremendous similarities in their choice of topics and contents and spirit. It may be noted that Al-Ghazali's influence on Aquinas has been documented by many authors. To quote Guillaume again: 'Among Algazel's work was a treatise on the place of reason as applied to revelation and the theologian dogmas. This work presents many parallels in its arguments and discussions with *Summa* of St Thomas, a fact which can hardly have more than one explanation" (Guillaume, 1931, p. 273).
24. Raymond Martini or Ramund Martin was a contemporary of St Thomas Aquinas. According to Arnold and Guillaume (1931, p. 273), his 'knowledge of Arabian authors has probably not been equalled in Europe until modern times.'

9. Conclusion

9.1 THE CHANGING SCENARIO

Highlighting the importance of economic teachings prevailing in Medieval Europe, O'Brien observes; 'No study of modern European economic thought can be complete or satisfactory unless it is based upon a knowledge of the economic teaching which was accepted in the Medieval Europe' (O'Brien, 1920, p. 1). We have tried to present well-documented evidence about historical linkages between the Arab-Islamic world and Medieval Europe, through the scholastic scholars. No study of economic teaching of Medieval Europe can be complete without acknowledging the contribution of the Muslim scholars.[1]

We have already noted Schumpeter's statement that Medieval Europe had to start in social sciences 'from little or nothing' (Chapter 7, section 7.3). Watt (1972, p. 2) is not hesitant to declare: 'For our indebtedness to Islam, we Europeans have a blind spot. We sometimes belittle the extent and importance of Islamic influence in our heritage, and sometimes overlook it altogether.' He reiterates: 'When about 1100 Europeans became seriously interested in the science and philosophy of their Saracen enemies, these disciplines were at their zenith; and the Europeans had to learn all they could from the Arabs, before they themselves could make further advances' (Watt, 1972, p. 43). Another scholar admits: 'What we call science arose in Europe as a result of a new spirit of inquiry, of new methods of investigation, of the methods of experiment, observation, and measurement, of the development of mathematics, in a form unknown to the Greeks. The spirit and those methods were introduced into the European world by the Arabs' (Briffault, 1928, quoted in Sharif, 1966, pp. 1355–6). Seen in this way, the pre-scholastic Muslim scholars' contribution is very strongly related to mainstream Western economics.

Translation of Greco-Arab and Islamic sources to European languages continued for about five centuries (by the end of the fourth century to the ninth century Hijrah corresponding with the eleventh century to the fifteenth century C.E.). Greek economic ideas which form the starting point of the European economic thought reached the West mixed with the Muslim scholars' commentary and addition.[2] Knowles admits: 'Beside acting as agents in the long process of transmitting Aristotelian thought from Syrian and Persian through Egypt to Spain, the Arabian thinkers handed over a legacy of their own to the Latins' (Knowles, 1963, p. 195). Ibn Rushd's (Averroes's) commentary on Aristotle's *Nichomachean Ethics* and *Politics* became popular in the West. In these books Aristotle gives his views relating to economics. Because of such an important role played by Arabic translations in Europe, Karl Pribram raises the question of 'how far the scholastics – as influenced by Arabian philosophers – misunderstood and misinterpreted the Aristotelian teachings' (Pribram, 1983, p. 633 footnote).

But translation was only one channel through which the Arab-Islamic thought reached the West. Many European scholars traveled to cultural capitals of the Islamic world, learned Arabic, studied under the Muslim teachers and returned to their countries to spread new ideas through writings and lectures. Trade and travel, war and peace, conquest and defeat, together living and departing, all helped in the transmission of ideas of the Muslim scholars as well as their exposition and interpretation of the Greek ideas. Certain Indian and Iranian sciences also filtered through them to Europe.

The Muslims had practical experience of dealing with the economy and state, spread over many centuries. Their ideas bore pragmatic orientation. The scope and subject matter of their economic thinking was not confined to only want satisfaction, economy of self-sufficient households, division of labor, barter and money. They discussed a host of other problems and developed several new ideas – an account of selected themes has been presented in the preceding chapters. As the Muslim scholars based their ideas on both the revealed knowledge and human reason, they were more suited to scholastic scholars who benefited from them to a greater extent. This is clear from the gap which is found between their voluminous body of thought on economic issues and almost no contribution of their predecessors, who could not have access to the Arabian sources. However, the war, hatred and rivalry hardly allowed them to acknowledge the debt of their benefactors. Unfortunately, the hangover from past antagonism still continues, which is manifest in retaining a gap in the history of economic thought by not investigating the missing link – which was obviously provided by the Muslim scholars.

9.2 RECOGNITION AND REHABILITATION

It is a matter of satisfaction that the situation is not altogether hopeless. There are Western scholars who have acknowledged the Muslims' contribution to science and culture in general and their role in development of economic thought in particular. It will be ungracious not to register their valuable remarks here. The French historian and educationist Sedillot, in his work published in 1854, repeatedly acknowledges the Arabs as the teachers of Europe.[3]

In 1876, R.B. Smith wrote in his work *Mohammed and Mohammedanism*: 'The dark age of Europe would have been doubly, nay trebly dark; for the Arabs who alone by their arts and sciences, by their agriculture, their philosophy, and their virtues, shone out amidst the universal gloom of ignorance and crime, who gave to Spain and to Europe an Averroes and an Avicenna, the Alhambra, and the Al-Kazar. . . . It was the Arabs who developed the sciences of agriculture and astronomy, and created those of Algebra and chemistry; who adorned their cities with colleges and libraries, as well as with mosques and palaces; who supplies Europe with a school of philosophers from Cordova, and a school of physicians from Salerno' (Smith, 1876, pp. 125–6; and 217). According to Carra de Vaux (1931, p. 377), the Muslim kept alive the higher intellectual life and the study of science at a time when the Christian West was fighting desperately with barbarism. Everyone in the West 'who had any taste for science, some desire for light turned to the East or to the Moorish West'.

In economics the ice was broken about 50 years ago[4] when Spengler authored 'Economic Thought of Islam: Ibn Khaldun'. He appreciated Ibn Khaldun's knowledge of economic behavior and remarked that 'one is compelled to infer from a comparison of Ibn Khaldun's economic ideas with those set down in Muslim moral philosophical literature that the knowledge of economic behavior in some circles was very great indeed, having been acquired through contact with cumulating experience, and that one must turn to the writing of those with access to this knowledge and experience if one would know the actual state of Muslim economic knowledge' (Spengler, 1964, p. 403). In another paper published in the *History of Political Economy,* Spengler (1971) held al-Biruni a forerunner of Malthus.

After a detail study of Ibn Khaldun's economic thought published in the *Journal of Political Economy*, Jean Boulakia concludes:

1. Ibn Khaldun discovered a great number of fundamental economic notions a few centuries before their official births. He discovered the virtues and the necessity of a division of labor before Smith and the principle of labor value before Ricardo. He elaborated a theory of population before Malthus and insisted on the role of the state on the economy before Keynes. The economists who discovered mechanisms that he had already found are too many to be named.

2. But, much more than that, Ibn Khaldun used these concepts to build a coherent dynamic system in which economic mechanisms inexorably lead economic activity to long-term fluctuations. Because of the coherence of his system, the criticisms which can be formulated against most economic constructions using the same notions do not apply here (Boulakia, 1971, p. 1117).

Finally she raises the question 'Should we retire the fatherhood of these economic concepts from the authors to whom they are attributed in our histories of thought?' (ibid.).

Karl Pribram, who died in 1973 and whose work was published posthumously had 'sought to provide the students and scholars of economics with a well-documented history of economic reasoning from the Middle Ages to the middle of the twentieth century', acknowledges the Muslim scholars' influence in a very clear and candid manner at various places in his work *A History of Economic Reasoning*, some of them we have already quoted in preceding pages. According to Pribram, knowledge and experience gained from the crusades played an important role in 'the consolidation of economic views in Europe' during the thirteenth century. But 'even more instrumental, perhaps, in promoting a new approach to economic problems was another fact: all relevant writings of the Greek philosopher Aristotle (384–322 BC) were gradually made available in Latin translations along with various treatises in which Arabian philosophers had interpreted Aristotle's work in the light of their own reasoning' (Pribram, 1983, p. 4).

Another scholar, Nicholas Rescher, states 'In the twelfth and thirteenth centuries, the first period of European impingement, Arabic philosophical writing exerted a significant simulative influence on the great synthesis Christians Aristotelianism by St Albert the Great and St Thomas Aquinas. This influence has not only been extensive and profound, but relatively continuous and astonishingly diversified' (Rescher, 1966, pp. 156–7). In fact, scholastics learned their principles from the Muslim scholars for 'the scholastic method used by medieval Christian scholastics was already in current use among Muslim jurists long before St Thomas' (Chejne, 1980, pp. 111–12).

Many researchers now have realized that any work on the history of economic thought will be incomplete if the Muslim scholars' contribution is not mentioned in such a work. They have, therefore, included in their edited volume or original writing a section or chapter on this aspect. In 1978 Marjorie Grice-Hutchinson authored *Early Economic Thought in Spain* in which she extensively wrote how Greek economics was developed and propounded by the Muslim scholars and how they transmitted it, along with their own original ideas, to the Christian West (1978, pp. 61–80). This has been one of our sources in the present study. In 1987 Lowry presented his excellent edited volume *Pre-Classical Economic Thought*, in which he has rightly assigned a place to 'Islamic Economic Thought' (Chapter 4) between 'Biblical and Early Judeo-Christian Thought' and 'Scholastic Economics' (1987, pp. 77–114).

In another edited volume, *Perspectives on the History of Economic Thought*, Volume 7, Lowry included two papers on aspects of Islamic economic thought; one on 'Greek Economic Thought in the Islamic Milieu: Bryson and Dimashqi' by Yassine Essid (1992, pp. 39–44) and another, 'Explorations in Medieval Arab-Islamic Economic Thought: Some Aspects of Ibn Taimiyah's economics' by S.M. Ghazanfar and A. Azim Islahi (1992, pp. 45–63). In 1994 Louis Baeck published *The Mediterranean Tradition in Economic Thought* in which he has extensively dealt with 'The economic thought of classical Islam and its revival' in one chapter (1994, pp. 95–124). This has been also an important source for the present work. These works show that the Islamic economic thought and the role played by the Muslim scholars and its place in development of mainstream economics are increasingly attracting attention of scholars and researchers. However, until at least a chapter is allocated on the Islamic economic thought in textbooks of economics, ignorance and misconception will persist. It is heartening that some writers are expressing their willingness to remove this deficiency of the textbooks. This is evident from the following extracts from letters of two authors of history of economic thought and analysis addressed to a former colleague of this writer:

Ingrid Rima wrote 'I want to let you know that the sixth edition of *Development of Economic Analysis* has tried to give better recognition to the importance of Arab-Islamic scholars' (IAFIE (2000), *Islamic Economics Bulletin*, 10 (6), 4, November–December). However, she could make only a brief reference to Islamic scholarship in the said edition (2001, p.10).

Harry Landreth wrote 'I . . . agree . . . that Schumpeter erred and that modern historians of economic thought have followed Schumpeter in failing to appreciate the Arab-Islamic writings in the approximately 500 years before Aquinas. . . . the failure of economists on this issue is part of a broader failure of Western scholars to fully understand the important contributions of Arab-Islamic scholars. I have a first draft of a rewrite of Chapter 2 and have added a new section entitled "Arab-Islamic Thought". . .' (IAFIE (2000), *Islamic Economics Bulletin*, 10 (6), 4). As promised he has included a section on Arab-Islamic thought in the latest edition and provided some references for the interested readers (Landreth and Colander, 2002, pp. 32–4). Islamic economics also attracted attention of Paul Gregory and Robert Stuart, who have discussed it in the seventh edition of their work *Comparing Economic Systems in the Twenty-First Century* (2004, pp. 31–4). No doubt, such developments will induce the researchers to bridge the gap in history of economic thought left by earlier writers. They will also increase understanding between the East and the West and facilitate interaction at academic and intellectual levels. Perhaps these were the feelings of Watt when he observed that 'For the sake of good relations with Arabs and Muslims we must acknowledge our indebtedness to the full. To try to cover it over and deny it is a mark of false pride' (Watt, 1972, p. 2). Intellectual integration is the call of the time.

We have seen above in Chapter 7 that the moral character of the human person and of his actions *per se*, was a constant concern of both the Muslim scholars and scholastic philosophers. Both considered justice, equity, common good, and protection of the weak as objectives of economic teachings and institutions. Both have talked about prohibition of usury, protection of the poor and the needy against exploitation, sharing risks, acceptance of just price, opposition of price fixation, condemnation of hoarding and monopoly, ban on forestalling and respect of human labor. No doubt, these common concerns in traditions of the East and the West can provide a basis for dialogue, promote cultural discussion and help in mutual understanding. They offer support for those who are in search of common grounds in sciences and culture and inter-civilization dialogue.

Needless to say, that since the era of scholastics and early Muslim scholars, the economic principles and practices have undergone drastic changes. Compositions of production and techniques have enormously developed. But man's nature remains the same. His conscience, ethics and human values have not changed. These were the overriding considerations in the period under our study. Deviation from those values would have adversely affected the social and economic environment. The recent world financial crisis has clearly shown that some of the main causes of the catastrophe were fraud, greed, seeking self-interest and risk shifting, absence of governance and lack of transparency on the part of market players.

Now that shortcomings of neo-classical economics are being blamed for the excesses of US-led globalization, due attention should be paid to the contribution of the Muslim scholars. It can secure two important purposes: first, coming from Asia and Africa, these voices represent concerns that are different from the European and American concerns. It is no secret that the East and its religions have always given precedence to equity, social justice, ethics and morality. Thus, it is hoped it would promote brotherly relations and human values among the nations. Second, it will lessen the dangers of the senseless clash of civilizations being trumped by some intellectuals in the West. We should pave the way for exchange and dialogue between the West and the East on an equal footing.[5] Indeed, through dialogue on the basis of tolerance and mutual respect, the shared values become more familiar than those that distinguish and divide.

NOTES

1. In a personal letter Professor Todd Lowry writes: 'The Medieval Europe got their economics served on an Islamic plate.' But this plate was substantially garnished by Arab scholarship (Ghazanfar, 2003, p. 20, footnote 5).
2. In his foreword of a recently published work Lowry observes: 'The torchbearer of ancient learning during the medieval period were the Muslims, and it was from them that the Renaissance was sparked and the enlightenment kindled. This has been amply demonstrated in the history of science and mathematics. What has been generally ignored, however, is the character and sophistication of Arabic writings on economic subjects' (Ghazanfar, 2003, p. xi).
3. The following are some of the passages from Sedillot's book *Histoire des Arabes,* authored in 1854, in which he acknowledges Europe's indebtedness to the Arabs:

> This people [the Arabs] raised high the flags of civilization in many lands at a time when Europe, in the shadow of ignorance during the Middle Ages, seemed to have forgotten its heritage of Roman and Greek civilizations.
>
> Their [the Arabs'] intellectual activities spread to all branches of human knowledge, resulting in remarkable creations which became well known in Europe. This shows beyond doubt that the Arabs were our teachers. They assembled the materials upon which our medieval history is based.
>
> They attained an unequaled peak in the industries, and the continued influence of their buildings also indicates the breadth of their knowledge. Likewise their extraordinary inventions give added evidence of their virtues which have not yet received the acclaim they deserve. If they made great advances in physics, natural history, chemistry and agriculture, although these sciences were among the tangible things which did not command their full attention, then one can imagine their progress in the rational sciences in which they exerted an effort beyond all limit from the beginning of the ninth century to the end of the fifteenth.
>
> In comparing what, as a result of our researches, we now know came from the Arabs with what remains unknown, it can be seen that in general the Arabs are the source of our knowledge. As we read their books we continue to come across things created by them which we formerly had attributed to others.
>
> Of all the nations in the Middle Ages only the Arabs were concerned with the sciences. Because of them the clouds of barbarism which had spread over a Europe shaken by the barbarian invasions were dispersed. The Arabs went back to search the ancient sources of wisdom. Nor were they content merely to preserve these treasures which they came across, but they strove to increase them and to open up new ways of contemplating their many marvels.
>
> Let us repeat that the productions and creations of the Arabs establish for us the marvellous ascendency of their intellectual activities in that epoch when their reputation extended to Christian Europe. This is proof that the Arabs, as others have said and I acknowledge, were our teachers.

These passages are noted from al-Tunisi's work *The Surest Path* (1967), pp. 108–11. For more details, one can refer to it.

4. In the modern period, the credit goes to Nicolas (son of) Prodromos Aghnides, a Turk of Greek origin, for writing the first work on a topic of Islamic economics – *Mohammedan Theories of Finance* – in 1916. It is a PhD dissertation from the Department of Political Science, Columbia University. The book is jurisprudential in nature which examines the opinions on financial matters in the four schools of *fiqh*.
5. Expressing similar concern, the Prince of Wales, in a lecture, observed: 'Western civilization has become increasingly acquisitive and exploitative in defiance of our environmental responsibilities. This crucial sense of oneness and trusteeship of the vital sacramental and spiritual character of the world about us is surely something important that we can learn from Islam' (the Prince of Wales, 1993, pp. 19–20).

References

ARABIC REFERENCES

Abd al-Jabbar, Qadi (1965), *al-Mughnī fī ʿAjāi'b al-Tawḥīd wa'l-ʿAdl*, edited by M. Ali Najjar and Halim Najjar, Cairo, al-Mu'assash al-Misriyah al- Ammah li'l-Talif.

Abu Dawud (n.d.), *Sunan Abi Dawud*, Beirut, al-Maktabah al-Asriyah, Vol. 3

Abu-Ubayd (1986), *Kitāb al-Amwāl*, Beirut, Dar al-Kutub al-Ilmiyah.

Abu-Yusuf (1392), *Kitāb al-Kharāj*, Cairo, Dar al-Matbaʿah al-Salafiyah.

Ahmad, Abd al-Rahman Yousri (2001), *Taṭawwur al-Fikr al-Iqtiṣādī*, Alexandria, al-Dar al-Jamiʿyah.

al-Aqṭash, Abd al-Majid Muhammad (1985), *Abu Dharr al-Ghifārī wa Arā'uhū fi'l-Siyāsah wa'l-Iqtiṣād* [*Abu Dharr and His Views on Political and Economic Issues*], Amman, Maktabah al-Aqsa.

al-Asadi, Muhammad b. Muhammad b. Khalil (1967), *al-Taysīr wa'l-Iʿtibār wa'l-Taḥrīr wa'l-Ikhtibār fī mā yajib min Ḥusn al-Tadbīr wa'l-Taṣarruf wa'l-Ikhtiyār*, edited by Abd al-Qadir al-Tulaymat, Cairo, Dar al-Fikr al-Arabi.

al-Asfahani, al-Husayn al-Raghib (1985), *al-Dharīʿah ilā Makārim al-Sharīʿah*, Cairo, Dar al-Sahwah; al-Mansurah, Dar al-Wafa.

Awwad, Sarkis (1943), 'al-Ḥisbah fī Khazānat al-Kutub al-Arabīyah' (works on *al-ḥisbah* in Arabian libraries), *Majallat al-Majmaʿ al-ʿIlmī al-ʿArabī*, **18** (1–2), 417–28.

al-Baji, Abu'l-Walid (1332 A.H.), *al-Muntaqā Sharḥ al-Muwaṭṭā* , Beirut, Dar al-Kitāb al-Arabi.

al-Baladhuri, Ahmad (1983), *Futūḥ al-Buldān*, edited by Muhammad Ridwan, Beirut, Dar al-Kutub al-Ilmiyah.

al-Bayhaqi, Abu Bakr Ahmad (1999), *al-Sunan al-Kubrā*, Beirut, Dar al-Kutub al-Ilmiyah, Vol. 5.

al-Burno, Muhammad Sidqi (1400 A.H.), *ʿUmar b. ʿAbd al-ʿAziz wa Taṣḥīḥātuhu li-Bayt al-Māl* [*Umar b. Abd al-Aziz and his Reforms of the Public Treasury*], Riyadh, Jāmiʿat al-Imām, Ph.D. Thesis.

al-Dimashqi, Abu'l-Fadl Jaʿfar (1977), *al-Ishārah ilā Maḥāsin al-Tijārah,* edited by al-Shorabji, Cairo, Maktabah al-Kulliyat al-Azhariyah.

Dunya, Shawqi Ahmad (1998), *Silsilah Aʿlām al-Iqtiṣād al-Islāmī*, Book III, Cairo, Markaz Salih Kamil li'l-Iqtisad al-Islami, pp. 19–63, 121–73.
al-Farra, Abu Yala (1966), *al-Aḥkām al-Sulṭānīyah,* Egypt, Al-Babi al-Halabi.
al-Ghazali, Abu Hamid (n.d.[a]), *'Iḥyā' ʿUlūm al-Dīn*, Beirut, Dar al-Nadwah.
al-Ghazali, Abu Hamid (n.d.[b]), *al-Mustaṣfā min Uṣūl al-Fiqh,* Beirut, Dar Sadir.
al-Ghazali, Abu Hamid (n.d.[c]), *Shifā al-Ghalīl,* Baghdad, al-Irshad Press.
al-Ghazali, Abu Hamid (1964), *al-Tibr al-Masbūk fi Naṣīḥat al-Mulūk*, translated and edited by F.R. Bagley as the *Book of Counsel for Kings,* Oxford, Oxford University Press.
al-Ghazali, Abu Hamid (1964), *Mīzān al-ʿAmal*, edited by Sulayman Dunya, Cairo, Dar al-Maʿarif.
al-Hashimi, Muhammad Yahya (1937), 'Naẓarīyat al-Iqtiṣād ʿind al-Bīrūnī' [*Economic Views of al-Biruni*], *Majallat al-Majmaʿ al-ʿIlmī al-ʿArabī*, (Damascus), **15** (11–12), 456–65.
Ibn Abd al-Salam, al-Izz (1992), *Qawāʿid al-Aḥkām,* Damascus, Dar al-Tabaʿah.
Ibn Abi al-Dunya (1990), *Iṣlāḥ al-Māl* [*Betterment of Wealth*], edited and published by Mustafa Muflih al-Qudah, al-Mansurah, Dar al-Wafa.
Ibn Abi al-Rabīʿ (1978), *Sulūk al-Mālik fī Tadbīr al-Mamālik*, Beirut, Turath ʿUwaydat.
Ibn al Athīr (1989), *Usd al-Ghābah,* Bierut, Dar al-Fikr.
Ibn al-Azraq (1977), *Badā'iʿ al-Silk fī Ṭabā'iʿ al-Mulk,* Baghdad, Wazarat al- Iʿlam.
Ibn Battutah, (1968), *Tuḥfat al-Nuẓẓār fī Gharā'ib al-Amṣār wa ʿAjā'ib al–Asfār,* Beirut, Dar al-Turath.
Ibn al-Hajj (1972), *al-Madkhal ilā Tanmiyat al-Aʿmāl bi Taḥsin al-Nīyāt*, Beirut, Dar al-Kitab al-Arabi.
Ibn Hanbal (n.d.), *Musnad*, Beirut, al-Maktab al-Islami.
Ibn Hazm (1347 A.H.), *al-Muḥallā*, Egypt, Matbaʿah al-Nahdah.
Ibn al-Humam, (n.d.), *Sharḥ Fat'ḥ al-Qadīr*, Cairo, al-Maktabah al-Tijariyah al-Kubra.
Ibn Jaʿfar, Qudamah (1981), *Kitāb al-Kharāj wa Ṣinā'at al-Kitābah*, Baghdad, Dar al-Rashid.
Ibn Jamāʿah (1987), *Taḥrīr al-Aḥkām fī Tadbīr Ahl al-Islām*, edited by Fu'ad Ahmad, Qatar, Presidency of the *Sharʿīyah* Court and Religious Affairs, 2nd edn.
Ibn al-Jawzi, Abd al-Rahman (1962), *Dhamm al-Hawā,* edited by Abd al-Wahid, Mustafa, n.p.
Ibn al-Jawzi, Abd al-Rahman (n.d.), *al-Shifā' fī Mawāʿiẓ al-Mulūk wa'l-*

Khulafā', edited by Fuad Abd al-Mun'im Ahmad, Makkah al-Mukarramah, al-Maktabah al-Tijariyah.

Ibn Khaldun (n.d.), *Muqaddimah,* Beirut, Dar al-Fikr.

Ibn al-Qayyim (1982), *Zād al-Maʿād*, edited by Shuʿayb al-Arnaut, Beirut.

Ibn al-Qayyim (1955), *I'lām al-Muwaqqiʿīn,* Cairo, Maktabah al-Saʿadah.

Ibn al-Qayyim (1953), *al-Ṭuruq al-Ḥukmīyah,* Cairo, Matbaʿah al-Sunnah al-Muhammadiyah.

Ibn al-Qayyim (1375 A.H.), *Madārij al-Sālikīn*, Cairo, al-Muhammadiyah.

Ibn Qudamah (1972), *al-Mughnī,* Beirut, Dar al-Kitab al-Arabi.

Ibn Rushd (1988), *Bidāyat al-Mujtahid*, Beirut, Dar al-Maʿrifah.

Ibn Taymiyah (1986) *Mukhtaṣar al-Fatāwā al-Miṣrīyah,* edited by Muhammad al-Ba'li, Dammam, Dar Ibn al-Qayyim.

Ibn Taymiyah (1976), *al-Ḥisbah fi'l-Islām,* Cairo, Dar al-Sha'b. English translation by Holland, Muhtar (1982), *Public Duties in Islam: The Institution of the Ḥisbah*, Leicester, The Islamic Foundation.

Ibn Taymiyah (1971), *al-Siyāsah al-Sharʿīyah,* Cairo, Dar al-Sha'b. English translation by Farrukh, Omar (1966*), Ibn Taimiya on Public and Private Laws in Islam*, Beirut, Khayats.

Ibn Taymiyah (1964), *al-Masā'il al-Mārdīnīyah,* Damascus, al-Maktab al-Islami.

Ibn Taymiyah (1963), *Majmūʿ Fatāwā Shaykh al-Islām Aḥmad Ibn Taymīyah*, edited by al-Najdi, Abd al-Rahman b. Muhammad, Al-Riyad, Matabiʿ al-Riyad.

Ibn al-Ukhuwwah (1938), *Maʿālim al-Qurbah fī Aḥkām al-Ḥisbah*, edited and translated by Ruben Levy, with Arabic text, London, Cambridge University Press.

al-Jāḥiẓ, ʿAmr b. Baḥr (1966), *Kitāb al-Tabaṣṣur bi'l-Tijārah*, edited by Abdul-Wahhab, Hasan Hasani, Tunis, Dar al-Kitāb al-Jadid.

al-Juwayni, Abd al-Malik (1400 H.), *al-Burhān fī Uṣūl al-Fiqh*, Cairo, Dar al-Ansar, 2nd ed., two parts in one volume.

al-Juwayni, Abd al-Malik (1981) *al-Ghayāthī*, edited by Abd al-Azim al-Deib, Cairo: Matbaʿah Nahdah Misr.

al-Juwayni, Abd al-Malik (1950), *al-Irshād ilā Qawāṭiʿ al-Adillah fi Uṣūl al-Iʿtiqad* edited by Musa, M. Yusuf and Abd al-Hamid, Ali Abd al-Munʿim, Cairo, Maktaba al-Khanji.

Kahf, Monzer (1995), *al-Nuṣuṣ al-Iqtiṣādīyah min al-Qur'an wa'l-Sunnah* [*Economic Texts from the Qur'an and Sunnah*], Jeddah, Markaz al-Nashr al-Ilmi, KAAU.

al-Kasani, Ala al-Din (n.d.), *Badā'iʿ al-Ṣanā'iʿ*, Cairo, Shirkat al-Matbu'at, al-Ilmiyah.

Khallaf, Abd al-Wahhab (1954), *Maṣādir al-Tashriʿ al-Islāmī fī mā lā Naṣṣ*

fīhi, Cairo, Maʿhad al-Dirasat al-ʿArabiyah al-ʿAlamiyah.
al-Kinani, Yahya b. Umar (1975), *Aḥkām al-Sūq,* edited by Abd al-Wahhab, Hasan Hasni, Tunis, al-Shirkah al-Tunisiyah li'l-Tawziʿ.
al-Maghribi, Abu'l-Qasim Husayn b. Ali (n.d.), *'al-Siyāsah'* in *Majmūʿ fi'l-Siyāsah*, edited by Fu'ad Abd al-Munʿim Ahmad, Alexandria: Mu'assasah Shabab al-Jamiʿah, pp. 35–60.
al-Maqdisi, Ibn Qudamah, Abd al-Rahman (1972), *al-Sharḥ al-Kabīr*, printed at the foot of *al-Mughnī* by Ibn Qudamah, Beirut, Dar al-Kitāb al-Arabi, 12 Vols.
al-Maqrizi, Muhammad Ali (1997), *Kitāb Durar al-Sulūk fī Siyāsat al-Mulūk*, al-Riyad, Dar al-Watan.
al-Maqrizi, Muhammad Ali (1983), *Naṣīḥat al-Mulūk*, edited by Khidr Muhammad Khidr, al-Sifah (Kuwait), Maktabat al-Falah.
al-Maqrizi, Muhammad Ali (1981), *Tas'hīl al-Naẓar wa Taʿjīl al-Ẓafar*, Beirut, Dar al-Nahdah al-Arabiyah.
al-Maqrizi, Muhammad Ali (1956), *Kitāb al-Sulūk,* Cairo, Lajnah al-Talif wa'l-Tarjamah, Vol. 2.
al-Maqrizi, Muhammad Ali (1940), *Ighāthat al-Ummah bi Kashf al-Ghummah*, Cairo, Lajnah al-Talif wa'l-Tarjamah.
al-Mawardi, Ali (1981), *Tas'hil al-Nazar wa Ta`jil al-Zafar*, Beirut, Dar al-Nahdah al-Arabiyyah.
al-Mawardi, Ali (1979), *Adab al- Dunyā wa'l-Dīn*, Beirut, Dar Iḥyā' al-Turath al-Arabi.
al-Mawardi, Ali (1973), *al-Aḥkām al-Sulṭānīyah,* Egypt, al-Babi al-Halabi.
al-Mawardi, Ali (1929), *Adab al-Wazīr*, Egypt, Maktabah al-Khanji.
al-Mawardi, Ali (n.d.), *al-Tuḥfat al-Mulūkīyah fi'l-Ādāb al-Siyāsīyah*, edited by Fu'ad Abd al-Munʿim. Alexandria, Mu'assasah Shabab al-Jamiʿah.
al-Misri, Rafic Yunus (1999), *Fi'l-Fikr al-Iqtiṣādī al-Islāmī:Qira'āt fi'l-Turath* [*On Islamic Economic Thought: Readings in the Heritage*], Jeddah, Markaz al-Nashr al-Ilmi, King Abdulaziz University.
al-Misri, Rafic Yunus (1981), *al-Islām wa'l-Nuqūd* [*Islam and Money*], Jeddah, International Center for Research in Islamic Economics, 2nd edn (1990).
Miskawayh (1964), *Risālah fī Māhīyat al-ʿAdl*, edited and translated by M.S. Khan, Leiden, Brill.
Miskawayh (n.d.), *Tahdhīb al-Akhlāq*, Cairo, al-Matbaʿah al-Misriyah.
al-Mawsili, Muhammad b. Muhammad b. Abd al-Karim (1416), *Kitāb Ḥusn al-Sulūk al-Ḥāfiẓ Dawlat al-Mulūk*, al-Riyad, Dar al-Watan.
al-Mubarak, Muhammad (1973), *Ārā' Ibn Taymīyah fi'l-Dawlah*, Beirut, Dar al–Fikr.
Muslim (n.d.), *Ṣaḥīḥ* , Cairo, Maktabah M. Ali Sabih, Vol. 5.

Nash'at, Muhammad Ali (1944), *al-Fikr al-Iqtiṣādī fī Muqaddimat Ibn Khaldūn* [*Economic Thought in the Prolegomena of Ibn Khaldun*], Cairo, Dar al-Kutub al-Misriyah.

al-Nawawi, Muhi al-Din (n.d.), *al-Majmūʿ,* edited by M.N. al-Mutiʿi, Jeddah, Maktabat al-Irshad.

Nuqli, Isam Abbas (1998), *Thabt: Bibliography* (contemporary Arabic works on history of Islamic economic thought), Jeddah, King Abdulaziz University.

Qalaʿji, Muhammad Rawwas (1408 A.H.), '*al-Fikr al-Iqtiṣādī ʿind ʿUmar bin al-Khaṭṭāb*' [*Economic Thinking of Umar bin Khattab*], *Majallah Markaz Buḥūth al-Sunnah*, **3**, 187–207.

al-Qurashi, Yahya b. Adam (1987), *Kitāb al-Kharāj*, Cairo and Beirut, Dar al- Shuruq.

al-Raḍī, al-Sharif (n.d.), *Nahj al-Balāghah min Kalām ʿAlī ibn Abī Ṭālib*, Cairo, Al-Istiqamah Press.

al-Rayes, Dia al-Din (1957), *al-Kharāj fī al-Dawlah al-Islāmīyah*, Cairo, Maktabah Nahdah Misr.

al-Rāzi, Fakhr al-Din (1938), *al-Tafsīr al-Kabīr*, Cairo, al-Matbaʿah al-Bahiyah.

Salih, Muhammad Zaki (1933), '*al-Fikr al-Iqtiṣādī al-ʿArabī fi'l-Qarn al-Khāmis ʿAshar*' [*Arab Economic Thought in the Fifteenth Century*], *Majallat al-Qānūn Wa'l-Iqtiṣād*, **3** (3), 15–360 and **3** (6), 755–809.

al-Ṣanaʿāni, Abd Al-Razzaq (1403 H.), *Muṣannaf Abd al-Razzāq*, Beirut, al-Maktab al-Islāmi, Vol.8.

Sezgin, Fuat (1984), *Muhādarāt fī Tarīkh al-ʿUlūm al-ʿArabīyah wa'l-Islāmiyah*, [*Lectures on Arabic and Islamic Sciences*], Frankfort, IGAIW.

Shalbi, Mahmud (1974), *Ishtirakīyatu ʿUthmān* [*Socialism of Uthman*], Beirut, Dar al-Jil.

al-Shāṭibi, Ibrahim (n.d.[a]), *al-Iʿ tiṣām*, Beirut, Dar al-Maʿrifah.

al-Shāṭibi, Ibrahim (n.d.[b]), *Al-Muwāfaqāt,* Cairo, al-Maktabah al-Tijariyah.

al-Shaybani, Muhammad b. Hasan (1986), *al-Iktisāb fi'l-Rizq al-Mustaṭāb*, Beirut, Dar al-Kutub al-Ilmiyah.

al-Shayzari, Abd al-Rahman b. Nasr (1407 H.), *al-Manhaj al-Maslūk fī Siyāsat al-Mulūk*, edited by Ali Abd-Allah al-Musa, al-Zarqa (Jordan), Maktabat al-Manar.

al-Shayzari, Abd al-Rahman b. Nasr (n.d.), *Nihāyat al-Rutbah fī Ṭalab al-ḥisbah* or *Aḥkām al-Ḥisbah*, Beirut, Dar al-Thaqafah.

al-Shirazi, Ibrahim (1976), *al-Muhadhdhab*, Cairo, al-Babi al-Halabi.

al-Sindi, Nur al-Din, (1986), *Ḥāshiyat al-Sindī ʿalā al-Nisā'ī*, edited by Abd al-Fattah Abu Ghuddah, Aleppo, Maktab al-Matbuʿat al-Islāmiyah, Vol. 7.

al-Subki, Taj al-Din Abu Nasr ʿAbd al-Wahhab (1978), *Muʿīd al-Niʿam wa Mubīd al-Niqam*, edited by David W. Myhram, New York, AMS Press. Reprint of the 1908 edn, London, Luzac.
al-Subki, Taqi al-Din Ali b. Abd al-Kafi (n.d.), *Fatāwā al-Subkī*, Beirut, Dar al-Maʿrifah.
al-Sunnami, Muhammad b. Awad (1986), *Niṣāb al-Iḥtisāb*, edited by Murayzan Saʿid Murayzan Asiri, Makkah, Maktabat al-Talib al-Jamiʿi.
al-Suyuṭi (1968), *Ḥusn al-Muḥāḍarah fī Mulūk Miṣr wa'l-Qāhirah*, Cairo, Dar Iḥyā' al-Kutub al-Arabiyah. Vol. 2.
al-Ṭarasusi, Ibrahim b. Ali (1992), *Tuḥfat al-Turk fī mā Yajib an yuʿmal fi'l-Mulk*, edited by Radwan al-Sayyid, Beirut, Dar al-Taliʿah.
al-Tirmidhi, Abu Isa (1976), *al-Jāmiʿ al-Ṣaḥīḥ* , Egypt, Mustafa al-Babi al-Halabi.
al-Tusi, Nizam al-Mulk (1961), *Siyasat Namah* translated by Hubert Darke, London.
al-WaṢabi, Muhammad b. Abd al-Rahman (1982), *al-Barakah fī faḍl al-Saʿy wa'l-Ḥarkah,* Beirut, Dar al-Marifah.
al-Zaylaʿi, Uthman (n.d.), *Tab'īn al-Ḥaqā'iq*, Beirut, Dar al-Marifah.
Ziadeh, Nicola, (1963), *al-Ḥisbah wa'l-Muḥtasib fi'l Islām*, Beirut, Catholic Press.

OTHER REFERENCES

Abdul-Qadir (1941), 'The Social and Political Ideas of Ibn Khaldun', *Indian Journal of Political Science*, **3** (2), 898–907.
Abulafia, D. (1994), 'The Role of Trade in Muslim Christan Contact during the Middle Ages', in D.A. Agius and R. Hitchcok (eds), *The Arab Influence in the Medieval Europe*, Reading: Ithaca Press, pp. 1–24.
Aghnides, Nicolas P. (1916), *Mohammedan Theories of Finance*, New York: Columbia University Press.
Ali, Abdullah Yusuf (1975) (translation and commentary), *The Holy Qur'an*, Leicester: The Islamic Foundation.
Ali, Abid Ahmed (1979) (translation), *Kitāb al-Kharāj by Abu-Yusuf*, Lahore: Islamic Book Centres.
al-Djazairi, S.E. (2005), *The Hidden Debt to Islamic Civilization*, Oxford: Bayt al-Hikma Press.
Anawati, Georges C. (1974), 'Philosophy, Theology and Mysticism', in J. Schacht (ed.), *The Legacy of Islam*, Oxford: The Clarendon Press.
Aquinas, Thomas (1947), *Summa Theologica*, New York: Benziger Brothers, II: II Q77 and Q78).

Artz, Frederick, B. (1953), *The Mind of the Middle Ages C.E. 200–1500: A Historical Survey*, New York: Aflred A. Knopf.
Asad, Muhammad (1980) (translation and explanation), *The Message of the Qur'an*, Gibralter: Dar al-Andalus.
Ashley, William J. (1893–1906), *An Introduction to English Economic History and Theory*, New York: G.P. Putnam and Sons, Vols 1 and 2.
Baeck, Louis (1994), *The Mediterranean Tradition in Economic Thought*, London and New York: Routledge.
Bates, Michael L. (1989), 'Crusade Coinage with Arabic Inscriptions, in Kenneth M. Satton (ed.), *A History of the Crusades*, Madison: University of Wisconsin Press, **6**, 421–82.
Bell, J.F. (1967), *A History of Economic Thought*, New York: The Ronald Press Company, 2nd edn.
Bernardelli, H. (1961), 'The Origins of Modern Economic Theory', *Economic Record*, 37, 320–38.
Boulakia, Jean David C. (1971), 'Ibn Khaldun: A Fourteenth Century Economist', *Journal of Political Economy*, 79 (5), 1105–18.
Briffault, R. (1928), *The Making of Humanity*, London: George Allen and Unwin Ltd.
Briffault, R. (1919), *The Making of Humanity*, London: George Allen and Unwin Ltd.
Burnett, Charles (1994), 'The Translating Activity in Medieval Spain', in Salma Khadra Jayyusi (ed.), *The Legacy of Muslim Spain*, Leiden: E.J. Brill, pp. 1036–58.
Carra de Vaux, Baron (1931), 'Astronomy and Mathmetics, in T. Arnold and A. Guillaume (eds) *The Legacy of Islam*, Oxford: Oxford University Press, 1st edn, pp. 376–97.
Chapra, Mohammad Umer (2009), 'The Global Financial Crisis: Can Islamic Finance Help?', in *Issues in the International Financial Crisis from an Islamic Perspective*, prepared by Group of Researchers, Islamic Economic Research Center, Jeddah: King Abdulaziz University.
Chejne, Anwar (1980), 'The role of al-Andalus in the movement of ideas between Islam and the West', in Khalil Semaan (ed.), *Islam and the West*, Albany: State University of New York Press.
Cochrane, Louise (1994), *Adelard of Bath*, London: British Museum Press.
Cook, M.A. (1974), 'Economic Developments', in J. Schacht and C.E Bosworth (eds), *The Legacy of Islam,* Oxford: The Clarendon Press, 2nd edn.
Copleston, F.C. (1972), *A History of Medieval Philosophy*, New York: Harper and Row.
Crowther, Geoffrey (1967), *An Outline of Money*, London: Nelson.

Dalton, Hugh (1966), *Principles of Public Finance*, London: Routledge & Kegan Paul.

Daniel, Norman (1975), *The Culture Barrier: Problems in the Exchange of Ideas*, Edinburgh: Edinburgh University Press.

al-Dawani, Jalal al-Din (1839), *Akhlāq-i Jalāli*, translated by W.F.Thomas, London: Oriental Translation Fund of Great Britain and Ireland.

de Roover, Raymond (1976), *Business Banking and Economic Thought*, Chicago and London: The University of Chicago Press.

Durant, Will (1950), *The Story of Civilization: The Age of Faith*, New York: Simon & Schuster, Vol. 4.

Ekelund (Jr.), Robert B. and Hebert, Robert F. (1983), *A History of Economic Theory and Method,* New York: McGraw-Hill.

Essid, Yassine (1995), *A Critique of the Origins of Islamic Economic Thought,* Leiden: E.J. Brill.

Essid, Yassine (1987), 'Islamic Economic Thought', in Lowry S. Todd (ed.), *Pre-Classical Economic Thought*, Boston: Kluwer Academic Publishers, pp. 77–102.

Fay, Charles (1956), *Adam Smith and Scotland of His Day*, Cambridge: Cambridge University Press.

Gabrieli, F. (1970), 'The Transmission of learning and Literary Influences to Western Europe', in P.M. Holt, A.K.S. Lambton and B. Lewis (eds), *The Cambridge History of Islam*, Cambridge: Cambridge University Press, Vol. 2, pp. 851–89.

Ghazanfar, S.M. (ed.) (2003), *Medieval Islamic Economic Thought*, London and New York: RoutledgeCurzon.

Ghazanfar, S.M. (1995), 'History of Economic Thought: The Schumpeterian Great Gap, The Lost Arab. Islamic Legacy and the Literature Gap', *Journal of Islamic Studies*, **6** (2), 234–53.

Ghazanfar, S.M. and Islahi, Abdul Azim (1998), *Economic Thought of al-Ghazali*, Jeddah, Scientific Publishing Centre, KAAU.

Ghazanfar, S.M. and Islahi, Abdul Azim (1990), 'Economic Thought of an Arab Scholastic: Abu Hamid Al-Ghazali', *History of Political Economy,* **22** (2), 381–403.

Goitein, S.D. (1967), *A Mediterranean Society*, Berkeley: University of California Press.

Gordon, Barry (1975), *Economic Analysis before Adam Smith,* New York: Barnes and Noble.

Gray, Alexander (1967), *The Development of Economic Doctrine*, London: Longmans.

Gregory, Paul A. and Robert C. Stuart (2004), *Comparing Economic Systems in the Twenty-First Century*, Mason: South-Western Cengage Learning, 7th edn.

Grice-Hutchinson, Marjorie (1978), *Early Economic Thought in Spain, 1177–1740*, London: George Allen & Unwin.
Hamdani, Abbas (1994), 'An Islamic Background to the Voyages of Discovery', in Salma Khadra Jayyusi (ed.), *The Legacy of Muslim Spain*, Leiden: E.J. Brill, 273–306.
Hamidullah, Muhammad (1968), *The Muslim Conduct of the State*, Lahore: Sh. Muhammad Ashraf, 5th edn.
Harris, C.R.S. (1954), *Duns Scotus*, New York: Humanity Press.
Haskins, Charles H. (1927), *The Renaissance of the Twelfth Century*, Cambridge, MA: Harvard University Press.
Hayes, J.R. (ed.) (1983), *The Genius of Arab Civilization: Source of Renaissance*, 2nd edn, Cambridge MA: MIT Press.
Heaton, Herbert (1948), *Economic History of Europe,* New York: Harper.
Heckscher, Eli F. (1954), *Mercantilism,* translated by Mendal Shapiro, London: George Allen and Unwin.
Heffening, W. (1934), '*Tadbīr*', in *The Encyclopaedia of Islam*, Old Edition, Leiden: E.J. Brill and London, Luzac and Co., Vol. 4, p. 595.
Hernandez, Miguel Cruz (1994), 'Islamic Thought in the Iberian Peninsula', in Salma Khadra Jayyusi (ed.), *The Legacy of Muslim Spain*, Leiden: E.J. Brill, pp. 777–803.
Hill, D.R. (1993), *Islamic Science and Engineering*, Edinburgh: Edinburgh University Press.
Hosseini, Hamid S. (2003), 'Contributions of Medieval Muslim Scholars to the History of Economics and their Impact: A Refutation of the Schumpeterian Great Gap', in Warren J. Samuels, Jeff E. Biddle and John B. Davis (eds), *A Companion to the History of Economic Thought*, Malden: and Oxford: Blackwell Publishing Ltd, pp. 28–45.
Hunter, M.H. and H.K. Allen (1940), *Principles of Public Finance*, New York: Harper and Brother.
IAFIE (2000), *Islamic Economics Bulletin,* Indian Association for Islamic Economics, **10**, 6.
Ibn Khaldun (1967), *Muqaddimah of Ibn Khaldun, (An Introduction to History),* translated by F. Rosenthal, New York: Princeton University Press.
Iqbal, Sir Muhammad (2006), *The Reconstruction of Religious Thought in Islam*, New Delhi: Kitab Bhawan (reprint edn).
Islahi, Abdul Azim (2011), *A Study of Muslim Economic Thinking in the 11th A.H./17th C.E. Century*, Jeddah: Scientific Publishing Centre, King Abdulaziz University.
Islahi, Abdul Azim (2011), *Islamic Economic Thinking in The 12th A.H./18th C.E. Century With Special Reference To Shah Wali-Allah*

Al-Dihlawi, Jeddah: Scientific Publishing Centre, King Abdulaziz University.

Islahi, Abdul Azim (2009), *Muslim Economic Thinking and Institutions in the 10th A.H./16th C.E. Century*, Jeddah: Scientific Publishing Centre, King Abdulaziz University.

Islahi, Abdul Azim (2008[a]), 'The Myth of Bryson and Economic Thought in Islam', *Journal of King Abdulaziz Uni*versity*: Islamic Economics,* Jeddah, (2008 C.E./1429 A.H.), **21** (1), 57–64.

Islahi, Abdul Azim (2008[b]), 'Thirty Years of Research on History of Islamic Economics: Assessment and Future Directions', in 'The 7th International Conference on Islamic Economics', Jeddah, Islamic Economics Research Center, pp. 347–69.

Islahi, Abdul Azim (2001), 'An Analytical Analysis of Al-Ghazali's Thought on Money and Interest', paper presented to the International Conference on Legacy of Al-Ghazali, organized by ISTAC, Kuala Lumpur, 24–27 October .

Islahi, Abdul Azim (1997), *History of Economic Thought in Islam: A Bibliography,* Jeddah: Scientific Publishing Centre, KAAU.

Islahi, Abdul Azim (1995), 'Islamic Distributive Scheme: A Concise Statement', in F.R. Faridi (ed.), *The Principles of Islamic Economics and the State of Indian Economy,* Aligarh: Indian Association For Islamic Economics, pp. 19–35.

Islahi, Abdul Azim (1988), *Economic Concepts of Ibn Taimiyah,* Leicester: The Islamic Foundation.

Islahi, Abdul Azim (1986), 'Ibn Taimiyah's Concept of Market Mechanism', *Journal of Research in Islamic Economics*, **2** (2), 55–66.

Islahi, Abdul Azim (1984), *Economic Thought of Ibn al-Qayyim*, Jeddah: International Center for Research in Islamic Economics.

Khan, Muhammad Akram (1989), *Economic Teachings of Prophet Muhammad* (pbuh), Islamabad: International Institute of Islamic Economics.

Knight, Frank H. (1955), 'Review article on *The History of Economic Analysis*, by Joseph A. Schumpeter', *Southern Economic Journal*, **21**, 261–72.

Knowles, David (1963), *The Evolution of Medieval Thought*, London: Longmans.

Kramers, J.H. (1965), 'Geography and Commerce', in S. Thomas Arnold and Alfred Guillaume, *The Legacy of Islam*, London: Lowe and Brydone Ltd (from the first edn 1931 reprinted).

Krueger, H.C. (1961), 'Economic Aspects of Expansionary Europe', in Marshal Claggett, Gaines Post and Robert Reynolds (eds), *Twelfth-*

Century Europe and Foundations of Modern Society, Madison: University of Wisconsin Press, pp. 59–76.

Kuran, Timur (1987), 'Continuity and Change in Islamic Economic Thought', in S. Todd Lowry (ed.), *Pre-Classical Economic Thought*, Boston: Kluwer Academic Publisher, pp.103–13.

Landreth, Harry and C. Colander David (2002), *History of Economic Theory,* Boston: Houghton Mifflin, 4th edn.

Lane-Poole, Stanley (1925), *A History of Egypt in the Middle Ages*, London: Methen and Co.

Langholm, Odd (1998), *The Legacy of Scholasticism in Economic Though*t, Cambridge: Cambridge University Press.

Langholm, Odd (1987), 'Scholastic Economics', in S. Todd Lowry, (ed.), *Pre-Classical Economic Thought*, Boston: Kluwer Academic Publishers, pp. 115–35.

Langholm, Odd (1979), *Price and Value in the Aristotelian Tradition,* New York: Columbia University Press.

Lewis, Bernard (1982), *The Muslim Discovery of Europe*, London: Weidenfeld and Nicolson

Lewis, Bernard (1970), 'Sources for the Economic History of the Middle East', in M.A. Cook (ed.), *Studies in the Economic History of the Middle East*, Oxford: Oxford University Press, pp. 78–92.

Lindberg, D.C. (1978), 'The Transmission of Greek and Arabic Learning to the West', in D.C. Lindberg (ed.), *Science in the Middle Ages*, Chicago and London: The University of Chicago Press, pp. 52–90.

Lipsey, Richard G. and Streiner, Peter O. (1981), *Economics,* New York: Harper International.

Lopez-Baralt, Luce (1994), 'The Legacy of Islam in Spanish Literature', in Salma Khadra Jayyusi (ed.), *The Legacy of Muslim Spain*, Leiden: E.J. Brill.

Lowry, S. Todd (ed.) (1992), *Perspectives on the History of Economic Thought*, Aldershot: Edward Elgar, Vol. 7.

Lowry, S. Todd (1987), *Pre-Classical Economic Thought*, Boston: Kluwer Academic Publisher.

Makdisi, George (2000),'The Reception of the Model of Islamic Scholastic Culture in the Christian West', in Ekmeleddin Ihsanoglu and Feza Gunergun (eds), *Science in Islamic Civilisation,* Istanbul: IRCICA.

al-Maqrizi, Muhammad Ali (1994), *Ighathat al-Ummah*, translated and edited by Adel Allouche as *Mamluk Economics,* Salt Lake City: University of Utah Press.

Mawdudi, S. Abul Ala (1963), 'Economic and Political Teachings of the Quran', in M.M. Sharif (ed.), *A History of Muslim Philosophy*, Karachi: Philosophical Congress, pp. 657–73.

McChesney, R.D. (1976), 'Ad-Dimashqi', in J.R. Hayes (ed.), *The Genius of Arab Civilization, Source of Renaissance*, Oxford: Phaidon.
Meyerhof, M. (1931), 'Science and Medicine', in T. Arnold and A. Guillaume (eds), *The Legacy of Islam*, Oxford: Clarendon Press, 1st edn, pp. 311–55.
Menocal, Maria Rosa (1985), 'Pride and Prejudice in Medieval Studies: European and Oriental', *Hispanic Review*, **53**, 61–78.
Metlitzki, D. (1977), *The Matter of Araby in Medieval England*, New Haven and London: Yale University Press.
Mirakhor, Abbas (1987), 'Muslim Scholars and the History of Economics: A Need for Consideration', *American Journal of Islamic Social Sciences*, **4** (2), 245–76.
Morison, Samuel E. (1963), *Journals and other documents on the life and voyages of Christopher Columbus*, New York: The Heritage Press.
Muir, S. William (1896), *The Mameluke or Slave Dynasty of Egypt*, London: Smith, Elder and Co.
Musgrave, R.A. and Musgrave, P.B. (1987), *Public Finance in Theory and Practice*, Singapore: McGraw-Hill.
Myers, Eugene A. (1964), *Arabic Thought and the Western World*, New York: Fredrick Ungar Publishing Company, Inc.
Nadvi, S. and Haq, Habibul (1976), '*al-Iqṭāʿ*', in *Contemporary Aspects of Economic Thinking in Islam*, Takoma Park:American Trust Publications, pp. 93–119.
Newman, Philip, et al., (1954), *Source Readings in Economic Thought*, New York: W.W. Norton.
O'Brien, George (1920), *An Essay on Medieval Economic Teaching*, London: Longman, reprint 1967.
O'Leary, De Lacy (1968), *Arabic Thought and its Place in History*, London: Routledge and Kegan.
Olson, Mancur (1982), *Rise and Decline of Nations*, New Haven: Yale University Press.
Oser, Jacob and Blanchfield, William C. (1975), *The Evolution of Economic Thought*, New York: Harcourt Brace, 3rd edn.
Perlman, Mark (1977), 'Introduction', in Joseph A. Schumpeter, *History of Economic Analysis*, London: Routledge.
Pribram, Karl (1983), *A History of Economic Reasoning*, Baltimore and Lord: The Johns Hopkins University Press.
The Prince of Wales (1993), *Islam and the West*, Oxford: Oxford Centre for Islamic Studies.
Rescher, Nicolas (1966), *Studies in Arabic Philosophy*, Pittsburgh, PA: Pittsburgh University Press.
Rifʿat, Syed Mubariz al-Din (1937), '*Maʿāshiyāt par Ibn Khaldun ke*

Khayālāt' (Ibn Khaldun's Views on Economics), *Maʿārif* (Azamgarh, India), **40** (1), 16–28; **40** (2), 85–95.
Rima, Ingrid H. (2001), *Development of Economic Analysis*, London and New York: Routledge, 6th edn.
Rima, Ingrid H. (1991), *Development of Economic Analysis*, Homewood: Richard Irwin, 5th edn.
Rodinson, Maxime (1974), 'The Western Image and Western Studies of Islam', in J. Schacht, and C.E. Bosworth (eds), *The Legacy of Islam*, Oxford: Clarendon Press, 2nd edn.
Roll, Eric (1974), *A History of Economic Thought*, Homewood: Richard D. Irwin Inc.
Rosenthal, F. (1967) (trans), *Muqaddimah of Ibn Khaldūn,* (An Introduction to History) New York: Princeton University Press, Vols 1, 2 and 3.
Rosenthal, E.I. (1965), *Averroes' Commentary on Plato's Republic,* Cambridge: Cambridge University Press.
Samuelson, Paul (1976), *Economics*, New York: McGraw-Hill Inc., 10th edn.
Samuelson, Paul and Nordhaus, William D. (2001), *Economics*, New York: McGraw-Hill, 17th edn.
Samuelson, Paul and Nordhaus, William D. (1985), *Economics*, Singapore: McGraw-Hill Inc., 12th edn.
Sanchez, Expiracion Garcia (1994), 'Agriculture in Muslim Spain', in Salma Khadra Jayyusi (ed.) (1994), *The Legacy of Muslim Spain*, Leiden: E.J. Brill, pp.987–99.
Sarton, G. (1924–1948), *Introduction to the History of Science*, Washington: The Carnegie Institute of Washington, Vols 1, 2 and 3.
Sauvaget, J. (1965), *Introduction to the History of the Muslim East: A Bibliographic Guide*, Berkeley: University of California Press, 2nd edn.
Schumpeter, Joseph A. (1997), *History of Economic Analysis*, London: Routledge.
Scott, William R. (1949), 'Greek Influence on Adam Smith', in *Études déchié es a la Memoire D'Andre' M. Andréaèds*, Athens: Prysos.
Semaan, K.I. (ed.) (1980), *Islam and the Medieval West*, Albany: State University of New York Press.
Sharif, M.M. (1966), *A History of Muslim Philosophy*, Weisbaden: Otto Harrassowitz, Vols 1 and 2.
Shemesh, A. Ben (1969) (trans.), 'Taxation in Islam' (Vol. III), in Abu Yūsuf, *Kitāb al-Kharāj*, Leiden: E.J. Brill and London: Luzac & Co.
Shemesh, A. Ben (1967) (trans.), 'Taxation in Islam' (Vol. I), in Yahya ben Adam, *Kitāb al-Kharāj*, Leiden: E.J. Brill (rev. edn).
Siddiqi, Muhammad Nejatullah (2008), 'Obstacles of Research in Islamic

Economics', in 'The 7th International Conference in Islamic Economics', Jeddah: King Abdulaziz University, pp. 3–12.

Siddiqi, Muhammad Nejatullah (1992), 'Islamic Economic Thought: Foundation, Evolution and Needed Direction', in Sadeq and Ghazali (eds), *Readings in Islamic Economic Thought*, Selangor: Longman Malaysia, pp. 14–32.

Siddiqi, Muhammad Nejatullah (1982), *Recent Works on History of Economic Thought in Islam – A Survey*, Jeddah: International Center for Research in Islamic Economics.

Siddiqi, Muhammad Nejatullah (1980), *Muslim Economic Thinking*, Jeddah: International Center for Research in Islamic Economics and Leicester, Islamic Foundation

Siddiqi, Muhammad Nejatullah (1964), '*Abū Yūsuf Kā Maʿāshi Fikr*' (Economic Thought of Abu Yusuf), *Fikr-o-Naẓar*, **5** (1), 66–95.

Smith, Adam (1937), *An Inquiry into the Nature and Causes of the Wealth of Nations*, New York: The Modern Library.

Smith, Margaret (1944), *Al-Ghazali the Mystic,* London: Luzac and Co.

Smith, R.B. (1876), *Mohammed and Mohammedanism*, London: Smith Elder.

Spengler, Joseph J. (1964), 'Economic Thought of Islam: Ibn Khaldun', *Comparative Studies in Society and History* (The Hague), **6**, 268–306.

Spengler, Joseph J. (1971), 'Alberuni: Eleventh-Century Iranian Malthusian', *History of Political Economy*, **3** (1), 92–102.

Tawney, R.H. (1938), *Religion and the Rise of Capitalism*, London: Penguin Books.

al-Tunisi, Khayr al-Din (1967), *The Surest Path* (English translation of *Aqwam al-Masālik fī Maʿrifat Aḥwāl al-Mamālik* by Leon Carl Brown, under the title *The Surest Path*), Cambridge: Harvard University Press.

al-Tusi, Nizam al-Mulk (1978), *Siyāsat Nāmah*, translated by Hubert Darke, London and Boston: Routledge and Kegan Paul.

Viner, Jacob (1978), *Religious Thought and Economic Society*, Durham: Duke University Press.

Watt, Montgomery, W. (1972), *The Influence of Islam on Medieval Europe*, Edinburgh: Edinburgh University Press.

Whittaker, Edmund (1960), *Schools and Streams of Economic Thought*, London: John Murray.

Wonnacott, P. and Wonnacott, R. (1986), *Economics*, Singapore: Mc-Graw Hill, 3rd edn.

Name index

Abbasid Caliphate (750–1517) 10, 49, 62
Abd al-Jabbar, Qadi 24
Abdul-Qadir
  'Social and Political Ideas of Ibn Khaldun, The' (1941) 2
Abrussan 18
Abu'l-'Ala, Salim 62
Abu Bakr 16
Abu Hanifah al-Nu'man, Imam 5, 8, 15
Abu Hanifah al-Nu'man b. Muhammad *see* al-Isma'ili
Abu Tufayl, Amir b. Wathila al-Kinani 15
Abu Ubayd al-Qasim bin Sallam 48, 51
Abu Yusuf, Yaqub b. Ibrahim 23, 45, 47–9, 53
  Kitāb al-Kharaāj 9, 44, 48
  opposition to tax farming 49
  proposed use of cost and benefit analysis in project development 52
  view on role of education in economic development 53
  views on funding of development projects 52
Adelard of Bath 76
Aghnides, Nicolas P. 102
Ahmad bin Hanbal *see* Ibn Hanbal
Albert the Great, St 65
  'Christian Aristotelianism' 98
de Albuquerque, Alfonso 72
Alexander III 66
Alfonso X, King
  court of 81
Alhazen *see* Ibn al-Haytham
Ali (Ibn Abi Talib) 26, 28
Ambrose 66
Ambrosius 64
Aquinas, St Thomas 65–7, 69, 84
  'Christian Aristotelianism' 98
  Summa 90
Aristotle 36–7, 62, 65–6, 72, 82–3, 90, 98
  definition of *nomisma* 37
  Nicomachean Ethics 14, 62, 76, 83, 96
  Politics 14, 83, 96
  rediscovery of works of 65–6, 68, 76
  view of trade 70
Artz, Frederick B. 80–81
al-Asadi, Muhammad b. Khalil 39, 43
al-Asfahani, al-Raghib 53
al-Ash'ari, Abu Masa 47
Ashley 90
Augustine, St. 64
Avenetan *see* Ibn al-Haytham
Avennathan *see* Ibn al-Haytham
Averroes *see* Ibn Rushd
Avicenna 97
Awwad 46, 49

Baeck, Louis 14, 75, 99
al-Baghdadi, Junayd 12
al-Baji, Abu'l-Walid Sulayman 27
Baldus 67
Barquq, al-Zahir 39
Baybars, Sultan Zahir 50–51
Bell, John Fred 82–3
al-Biruni 97
al-Bitriq, Yahya b. 62–3
Boulakia, Jean 97–8
Bryson 11, 16, 18
Burnett, Charles 14

Charlemagne 80
Charles IV of France, King 80
Charles the Bald 81
Chrystomus 64
Colbert, Jean Baptiste 72
Columbus, Christopher 71

Ibn al-Haytham, Al-Hasan b. Husayn, 11. 17
Ibn Hazm 51
Ibn al-Humam 41
Ibn Ja'far, Qudamah 36, 42, 48
Ibn Jaldun 5 *see* Ibn Khaldun
Ibn Jama'ah
  Tahrīr al-Ahkām fī Tadbīr Ahl al-Islām 44
Ibn al-Jawzi, Abd al-Rahman b. Ali 21, 28
Ibn Jubayr 79
Ibn Khaldun 2, 22, 26, 31, 34, 36, 47–8, 50, 54, 62
  influence of 97–8
  Introduction 30
  Muqaddimah 31
  students of 25, 56
  theories of supply and demand 25–6
  theory of development 54–6
  'asabīyah 55
  role of population size in 55–6
  theory of wages 33–4
  view of role of real estate 34
Ibn al-Khatib, Lisan al-Din, (Ibn al-Jatib in Spanish) 58
Ibn al-Khattab, Umar, the second Caliph 9, 15, 26, 36, 49
Ibn al-Muqaffa, Abd Allah b. al-Mubarak 23, 28, 58
Ibn Marwan, Abd al-Malik 9, 16
Ibn Nujaym 93
Ibn Qalawun, Sulan Nasir Muhammad 49–50, 80
Ibn al-Qayyim 25, 41
Ibn Qudamah 33
Ibn Qutaybah 57
Ibn Rajab 48
Ibn Randaqah *see* al-Turtushi
Ibn Rushd (Averroes) 13, 14, 37, 97
  commentaries on Aristotle 62, 76, 83
Ibn Sina. See Avicenna
Ibn al-Taqtaqa 59
Ibn Taymiyah 24–6, 45, 47, 51–2, 62
  fatāwā 41
  al-Hisbah fi'l-Islām 25
  observations of impact of counterfeiting/debasement of currency 39–40
  recommended punishment for not sharing 68
  al-Siyāsah al-Shar'īyah 44, 49–50
  students of 25
  view of function of money 37
  view of 'just price' 26–7
  view of role of prohibition of interest 41
  view of wages 33
Ibn Tufayl 11
Ibn al-Ukhuwwah 45
Ibn Wahshiyah, Abu Bakr b. Ali
  Kitāb al-Filāhah 30
Ibn Walid, Khalid 9, 16
Ibn Wushmagir, Qabus 57
Ibn Yazid, Khalid 9, 16
Ibn-Zanjawayh 9, 16, 48
al-'Ijli, Abu Dulaf al-Qasim b. Isa b. Idris 57
al-Isma'ili, Abu Hanifah al-Nu'man
  Da'ā'im al-Islām 44
al-Iskafi, Abd-Allah 57

al-Jahiz
  al-Tabass ur bi'l-Tijārah [*Insight in Commerce, The*] 23–4
James the Conqueror, King 81
al-Jarsifi 45
al-Jawzi, Ibn 21
al-Jilani, Abd al-Qadir 12
John XXII, Pope 71, 80
de Joinville, Jean
  memoirs of 79
al-Juwayni, Abu al-Ma'ali Abd al-Malik 21, 24
  students of 24

al-Kasani, Ala al-Din Abu Bakr b. Mas'ud 23
Kaus, Kay
  Qabūs Nāmah 44
Keynes, John Maynard 11, 97
al-Khallal, Abu Bakr 9
Khusraw, Nasir 79
al-Kinani, Yahya bin Umar 10, 27
al-Kindi 11
Knight, Frank 5
Knowles, David 95–6
Kramers, J.H. 67

Subject index

al-'afw (surplus) 67, 74n
agoranomos 46, 69, 78
agriculture/farming 9–10, 53, 78, 97
  as economic activity 29, 49
  perceived importance of 29–30
  proposed taxation of 23, 49
  supply of product 23
Arabic (language) 2, 37, 76, 79
  translation of works into/from 7, 9, 13–14, 45, 75–6, 88, 96
  Western terms originating in 69–70
Athenian economy 83

banking and finance 83
bartering exchange 41, 61, 96
  difficulties of 36–7
Bay' al-'īnah, 60
Bay' al-mudtarr 66
Bedouins 30
Black Death 88
borrowing 40, 48, 51, *see also* public borrowing

cost 20, 22, 25, 26, 33, 34, 38, 72
Cameralism 82
capital 22, 32, 40
  human 30
capitalism 82, 84
classical economics 22
Colbertism 82
commenda see also muḍārabah 67, 68, 78
communism 68
competition 17, 27
cooperation 30–31
competitive market forces 27
cost and benefit analysis 52
credit 9, 25
Crusades 70–72, 78, 79

deficit financing 51
demand 9, 11, 17, 21, 24–6, 31, 32, 34
  elastic 25
  inelastic 25, 27
demographic theory 55
  development 44, 45, 47, 53–6, 59, 60, 61
distribution 31–2
  functional 31–2
  initial 31
disutility
  concept of 21
division of labor 18, 24, 30, 31, 61, 62, 96, 97
dīwān 9

economic analysis 1–2
economic development
  cyclical model of 54
    conquest and success 54
    content and compromise 54–5
    economic prosperity 54–5
    extravagance 54–5
    stability and self-exalting 54
  relationship with public finances 56
  role of education in 53
  sustainable 53
economic efficiency 62, 68
economic thought
  'great gap' in evolution and development of 2–3, 64
economic welfare 47, 68
education
  role in economic development 53
extravagance 51, 54, 55, 63, 68

fiscal policy 9
forestalling [*talaqqī al-jalab*]
  religious prohibition against 69